Praise

Make Every Day Meaningful

"Realizing, recording, and remembering life's grand lessons has strengthened my faith, enhanced my ability to see and receive miracles in my life, and helped me to see the Lord's hand in my daily life. I am delighted that Randal is now sharing some new recording and remembering tools with all of us to help us live every day with more meaning and awareness. I highly recommend this book."

—**Brydon Brett**, author of *The Artist-Disciple*; singer and songwriter with "The Bretts" in Branson, MO

"Randal Wright has the rare ability to cut through irrelevant minutia and find the issues that really matter. With a beautiful combination of broad reading, principle-centered education, common sense, and humor, Randal shares those life-changing practices that will have the most enduring value. Whenever I read or listen to something from him, I am motivated to change, and I have been given simple but profound instructions on how to make those changes realities in my life. The same is absolutely true for this book on recording lessons from life. I wouldn't miss this book or anything Randal writes or teaches!"

—**Shon Hopkin**, PhD; assistant professor of Ancient Scripture at BYU; speaker for EFY and Campus Education Week

"Is there anything more priceless we can leave our loved ones, along with the generations that follow, than our written words? No! We may think we have nothing important to share, but I promise we all have something important to share. Read this thought-provoking book on recording life's grand lessons by Randal Wright and you will be inspired to begin this most rewarding journey of recording your experiences and memories. By doing so, you will make every day more meaningful."

—**Brenda Birrell**, founder of Pebbles in My Pocket

"Randal Wright's name is truly an inspiration . . . to write! Within each page of his newest book, Randal encourages us to be modern-day treasure hunters, discovering new ideas every day and then recording what we learn. Randal's fascinating stories remind us that we can find great meaning in our lives through simple moments and reflection. What an enriching goldmine this book is!"

—**Trina Boice**, author of *My Future Is So Bright I Gotta Wear Shades* and *How to Stay Up in a DOWN Economy*

"As an avid writer and journal keeper, I found Randal Wright's book both inspiring and uplifting. His three-word method for tracking and retaining experiences is apt for today's digital-heavy society. I can't wait to try it. Even better, Wright goes beyond method and draws out the reasoning for why our personal record keeping can enhance all areas of our lives. As with his other books, the stories and anecdotes are funny, poignant, and leave the reader with a desire to pull out that journal and start writing."

—**Tiffany Gee Lewis**, freelance journalist for the *Deseret News* and *Mormon Times*

"I was meant to read this powerful book because I needed it! Randal Wright has not only taught the key to making every day of our lives more meaningful, he has shown us how. In the way that he does best, Randal Wright teaches life-changing truths by revealing the principles in compelling stories. But most important, he shows us how we can all do the same by drawing on our everyday experiences to learn and be changed for the better."

—**Jenet Jacob Erickson**, PhD; teacher at the School of Family Life at BYU; columnist for the *Deseret News*

"Randal Wright has created a simple yet effective way to capture life's meaningful experiences. His effortless tool has allowed us to remember cherished moments with just a minute's worth of time. As Heartbound, we meet the most incredible people whom we share some of life's most tender moments and we want to always remember them. This efficient method has allowed us to have them indelibly impressed upon our memory forever."

—**Heartbound (Lori Hales, Debbie Bastian, and Me'Chel Musgrave)**, www.heartboundmusic.com

MAKE Every Day
MEANINGFUL

RANDAL A. WRIGHT

MAKE Every Day

MEANINGFUL

Realize, Record, and Remember
LIFE'S GRAND LESSONS

CFI
An Imprint of Cedar Fort, Inc.
Springville, Utah

ISBN 13: 978-1-4621-1470-2

Published by CFI, an imprint of Cedar Fort, Inc.
2373 W. 700 S., Springville, UT 84663
Distributed by Cedar Fort, Inc., www.cedarfort.com

LIBRARY OF CONGRESS CATALOGING-IN-PUBLICATION DATA

Wright, Randal A., author.
Make every day meaningful / Randal A. Wright.
    pages cm
Includes bibliographical references.
Summary: Discusses how to find joy in daily life.
ISBN 978-1-4621-1470-2 (alk. paper)
1. Christian life--Mormon authors. 2. Diaries--Authorship--Religious aspects. 3. Autobiography--Religious aspects--Church of Jesus Christ of Latter-day Saints. 4. Mormons--Conduct of life. I. Title.

BX8656.W75 2014
248.4'89332--dc23

2014018826

Cover design by Shawnda T. Craig
Cover design © 2014 Lyle Mortimer
Edited and typeset by Kevin Haws

Printed in the United States of America

10 9 8 7 6 5 4 3 2 1

Printed on acid-free paper

CONTENTS

Introduction 1

Chapter 1: The Necessity of Recording Meaningful Lessons 5

Chapter 2: Seeing the Hand of the Lord in Your Life 15

Chapter 3: The Necessity of Recording Family Stories 27

Chapter 4: Learning Meaningful Lessons from Others 41

Chapter 5: How to Use Your Grand Lessons 53

Chapter 6: Three-Word Summaries to Scripture Verses 69

Chapter 7: Search, Ponder, and Pray 81

Chapter 8: A House of Learning 95

Chapter 9: A Protection from Serious Mistakes 107

Chapter 10: Overcoming Weaknesses That Limit You 117

Chapter 11: Learn to Be Grateful Every Day 129

Chapter 12: Meaningful Lessons Are Not Lost 141

Chapter 13: Writing Your Autobiography 161

Chapter 14: Make Every Day Meaningful 175

Notes 177

About the Author 183

INTRODUCTION

Harvey Cluff: "No intelligent person in youth or old age should merely drift along. Look the world squarely in the face, listen and learn and not pass along, in life, indifferently, *for there are grand lessons before you every minute.*"[1]

When I turned nineteen, the Vietnam War was raging. The government had reinstituted a policy that allowed only two missionaries to be called per year in each ward. With my birthday being at the end of the year, I was drafted and served two years active duty. After my military release, I enrolled at Lamar University but had a strong desire to attend Brigham Young University. Three semesters later, the time came and I transferred. It turned out to be a very lonely semester since, at that time, I was seriously dating my future wife, Wendy. She continued at Lamar that semester but applied and was accepted to BYU for later that year, in the fall semester. That summer, we were married and immediately moved to Provo to continue our education.

Wendy had joined the Church when she was eighteen and was very excited to be taught by faithful Latter-day Saint professors. I was especially excited that we were going to be taking a Book of Mormon class together. I had learned much from Ivan J. Barrett—a popular Book of Mormon teacher and author—the previous semester. The class was huge and taught in the Joseph Smith Auditorium. I couldn't wait for Wendy to be taught by someone like Brother Barrett.

We didn't get into Brother Barrett's class that fall, but I was confident that anyone who taught in the religion department would be fantastic. What I didn't realize is that there are not enough religion professors to teach all of the classes that fulfill BYU's religion requirements. To solve this, the university asks other departments to supply teachers to meet the need. So a professor of religion may actually be from the biology department. Or, in our case, it was a staff member who worked in the administration building.

That Book of Mormon class turned out to be the worst class I ever took at BYU. The teacher was a nice man, but he knew little on the subject. During each class, a Book of Mormon was passed around and students read several verses at a time. After finishing a section, the teacher gave us an opportunity to discuss it, and then we read some more. Of course, we had some good readers and not-so-good readers, which made each class unmemorable to say the least.

Even though it was the worst class I had at BYU, that class also changed my life. I will forever be grateful that my wife and I took that class. In it, I made a vow that I would never have a teacher like that again. So I got a little notebook and started asking students this question: "Who is the best teacher you've taken at BYU?" Through this process, I learned who were their favorite teachers and what they taught. I didn't just want the best religion professors; I wanted the best in all of my required subject areas. My goal was to make every single day a meaningful one. Before long, my little book listed the names of outstanding professors in multiple departments. For example, George Pace, Leon Hartshorn, Ivan J. Barrett, Robert J. Matthews, Cleon Skousen, and David Yarn were said to be the best instructors available. In other departments, I heard names like Arthur Bassett in Humanities, Reed Bradford in Sociology, and Stephen R. Covey in Organizational Behavior. Whatever department I had to take a class in, I had my list of recommended professors.

I would often suggest to my brother Jack that he attend my morning classes with me. At that time, he had a BS degree from BYU and was working on his Master's degree. I still remember the day he took me up on it and came to my morning classes with me. We started off in my Old Testament class with Cleon Skousen. He had a law degree from George Washington University and was a former FBI agent, the former police chief of Salt Lake City, and an author of multiple books. He was an amazing teacher who had his classes mesmerized as he taught. Next, we attended my sociology class, taught by Reed Bradford. He had a Harvard PhD and had been voted one of the top ten professors in the first 100 years of BYU. It was interesting how he could make the Savior the focal point of every sociology class. He was also without a doubt the best storyteller I had ever heard. As one of his former students said, "People would be in a trance when he started telling stories." After that we went to my organizational behavior class with Stephen R. Covey. He taught us some of the same principles he later used in his hugely successful book, *7 Habits of Highly Effective People*.

After those three classes, Jack and I were talking outside the Jesse Knight Building. He said, "I have wasted my entire time at BYU." He went on say that he had no idea teachers like that even existed. He had paid no attention to the many options of teachers offered and had just randomly picked every class. I was so grateful that day for the Book of Mormon class I took with Wendy. In various ways, it not only changed my BYU experience, but it also changed my life. Not only did I try to look for the classes that I thought would be most meaningful, I also started looking for experiences and observations that would make every day meaningful.

However, even the most memorable days can be quickly forgotten. During our second year at BYU together, I had another life-changing experience. The night our first child was born, I was sent to the waiting room in the Utah Valley Hospital while my wife had an emergency C-section. I was so afraid and, while sitting there waiting, I made a commitment. I vowed that every day for the rest of my life I would look for meaningful experiences and observations to teach me lessons. I also vowed to record those lessons so I would not forget them and could then pass them on to my posterity.

I believe that one day we will be asked to turn in accounts of the meaningful experiences we've had during our earthly mission. I base that belief on the teachings of latter-day prophets and apostles. Consider for example this editorial written in the *Millennial Star*, edited by Parley P. Pratt:

> *Do you keep a Journal?* If so, well—and you will have your reward; and if not, we would again enjoin it upon you, and upon all who have not before heard the admonition, to commence forthwith to keep a Journal, or write a history; and see to it, that what you write is strictly true and unexaggerated; so that in the end, all may know of all things concerning this last work, and all knowledge may flow together from the four quarters of the earth, when the Lord shall make his appearing, and we all may be ready to give a

full account of our mission, our ministry and stewardship, and receive the welcome tidings, "Thou hast been faithful over a few things, I will make thee ruler over many things; enter thou into the joy of thy Lord."[2]

This book is an attempt to help readers look closely at life in order to discover grand lessons every day. My hope is that we will not only recognize these lessons as they occur but that we will also record them for our personal benefit and for the benefit of our posterity. None of us know exactly how much time we have left on earth. It could be years from now or it could be today. The one thing we do know is that "this life is the time for men to prepare to meet God; yea, behold the day of this life is the day for men to perform their labors" (Alma 34:32). By waking up every morning with a desire to make the day meaningful, we will be prepared to give a full account of our mission, ministry, and stewardship when the Savior comes again.

Notes

1. Harvey Cluff Autobiography, typescript, BYU–S, 8 (italics added).

2. The *Millennial Star*, No. 6, Vol. 1, Oct. 1840, 160–61.

CHAPTER 1
The Necessity of Recording Meaningful Lessons

Oliver Huntington: "Like men in general I presume to suppose, that I shall have a posterity; and that may; like me; wish to know of their father's life, that they might view it, and perhaps profit thereby, or at least, have the satisfaction of knowing it. This is one object that induces me to write; that my nearest kindred, might know of their kinsman. I write also for a satisfaction to myself, to look over my past life, dates and events, and to comply with a requirement, oft repeated by the prophet Joseph Smith, 'That every man should keep a daily journal.'"[1]

On the Sunday afternoon of June 25, 2000, I visited the cemetery in Vidor, Texas, where my great-grandparents William and Joissine Williamson are buried. Sitting on the ground near their tombstones, I hoped to receive inspiration for the talk I would present that night in the Orange Texas Stake Center to celebrate the hundredth anniversary of this couple's baptism.

William had been born in 1829 and Joissine in 1838, both in Louisiana. In 1866, they moved to southeast Texas after William finished his service as a Civil War soldier. Joissine was a multi-generation Catholic, but after moving to Texas she joined the Baptists as there were no Catholic churches in the area. Several of her children followed her decision and became members of the Baptist church. William, however, refused to join any church, believing all preachers needed the authority from God to preach.

The winter of 1900 brought two Mormon missionaries, Elders James G. Reed and Joseph A. Brooks, up the long lane leading to the Williamsons' home. William, now seventy years old, happened to look out the window as they approached and said, "Them's my men!" Elder Brooks made the following entry in his journal concerning that day:

> Tues., 9 Jan. 1900—The lady [Mrs. Weiss] started us out on a road but we got lost. We could not see the sun so lost our direction but finally came out all right. We came to a place. The man's name was Williamson. He was a very nice old gentleman. This was about dinner time. We took dinner with him. He asked us if we would not stop and preach for them that night. We had got a little out of our county and into Orange County but we told them that we would preach. We had a very good time.

A few months after their initial contact, the missionaries returned and both William and Joissine were baptized near their home. Their baptisms marked the beginning of the Church in southeast Texas. William passed away just a few months later, but Joissine lived to see a log church built in 1901—the first LDS Church building in the area—and a Sunday School organized in 1902. She died less than two years before the Williamson Branch was organized on January 29, 1914. Ultimately, all nine of their surviving children were baptized and, at this writing, William and Joissine have approximately five thousand descendants. Currently, four wards bear the name Williamson and meet in the Williamson chapel, located a short distance from where the couple was baptized.

That day in the cemetery, I was filled with gratitude for their willingness to accept the gospel message and be baptized. I scanned over the names of all fifteen of their children that were listed on the tombstones. I was sad to see the names of six children who died before their parents: at four months, seven months, three years, six, eleven, and twenty-five. At the same time, I was so grateful that my great-grandparents had the courage to continue having children because my grandmother Epsie was their fifteenth and last child. She followed her parents' examples and was also baptized in 1900.

I still remember looking at my great-grandfather's name on the tombstone that day and silently asking him, "Well, Grandpa, what do you want me to say to your descendants tonight?" Almost immediately, an unexpected thought came: *Tell them I'm sorry.*

I was shocked by this thought. Many of his descendants and their spouses had served missions, been Relief Society presidents, bishops, stake presidents, and mission presidents. Wondering what he could possibly be sorry for, another thought came into my mind: *Tell them I'm sorry I didn't keep a record of my life to leave to my posterity. Tell them I'm sorry I didn't even take the time to write down my own father's name or where he was born. Now my descendants have spent years, countless hours, and thousands of dollars trying to find out anything about him.*

That night I spoke in a stake center full of Williamson descendants and shared with them the experience I'd had earlier that day at the cemetery. I also told them that I believed the real message he was trying to communicate to his posterity was that they should not make the same mistake he had made. Consider the treasure our family would have if he had recorded his life experiences. Imagine reading how he felt when his mother died, leaving him an orphan at age thirteen, or his experiences fighting in the Civil War. How did he and his wife deal with the deaths of six of their children? But because he neglected to keep a record, those experiences—and the lessons to be learned from them—are now buried six feet under in a cemetery that bears his name.

Joseph Smith spoke of the deep regret he felt for neglecting to keep careful records early in his ministry. He said, "We have neglected to take minutes of such things, thinking, perhaps, that they would never benefit us afterwards; which, if we had them now, would decide almost every point of doctrine which might be agitated. But this has been neglected, and now we cannot bear record to the Church and to the world, of the great and glorious manifestations which have been made to us with that degree of power and authority we otherwise could, if we now had these things to publish abroad."[2]

Many people, even prophets, have difficulty recording the important lessons they observe or experience in life, losing knowledge that could be of infinite importance. Even some in the Church with specific responsibilities for personal and family history seem to struggle with this counsel. In September 2010, I attended our ward priesthood meeting where we discussed the importance of keeping written records. During the lesson, the instructor asked the twenty-eight high priests in attendance to raise their hands if they kept a

consistent written record of their lives. Only two hands went up that day. Reasons for not doing so included:
- I've never enjoyed writing
- I'm too busy
- I have nothing important to write
- I don't want to be reminded of the past
- I'm not a good writer
- I don't really see the purpose

Mine was one of the two hands raised that day. This is not to boast in any way but only to express the great desire I have developed over the years to leave a written record of the important lessons I learned in life and how those lessons can make each day meaningful. I have now recorded approximately five thousand experiences and observations that have made my life more meaningful during the past forty years.

What motivated me to do this? It was that promise made in a waiting room at the Utah Valley Hospital in Provo, Utah. Alone that night, I fervently prayed for the safety of my wife and first child. I promised Heavenly Father that if He would protect my wife and child, I would record the important lessons from my life. I also swore to teach my posterity and others what I learned.

Wilford Woodruff best explained why so few keep detailed records: "We are not apt to think of the importance of events as they transpire with us, but we feel the importance of them afterwards. We are living in one of the most important generations that man ever lived on earth, and we should write an account of those important transactions which are taking place before our eyes."[3] That statement has helped me to get up every day with a question on my mind as I observe and experience the world around me. The question: "What lesson can I learn from this? How can I use it to make every day meaningful?" Each day I'm like a kid on an Easter egg hunt, except my eggs are lessons learned.

Since the Church was first organized, Latter-day prophets have counseled the Saints to keep records. Yet the vast majority seems to have not followed that counsel. Maybe it's because we don't understand why personal records should be kept and it's hard to motivate ourselves to do it. President Spencer W. Kimball, a meticulous record keeper, pointed out the ultimate reason why we should do so.

Make Every Day Meaningful

Keep journals and family records. Let us then continue on in this important work of recording the things we do, the things we say, the things we
think, to be in accordance with the instructions of the Lord. For those of
you who may not have already started your books of remembrance and
your records, we would suggest that this very day you begin to write your
records quite fully and completely. We hope that you will do this, our
brothers and sisters, for this is what the Lord has commanded.[4]

Imagine that since your early teens you have had a goal of getting into to the Yale University Law School. So you work extremely
hard in high school and during your undergraduate years to prepare.
Before taking the LSAT, you go through an expensive prep course
and multiple practice exams to increase your chances of doing well.
Finally, after years of preparation, you apply and are thrilled to be
one of the 6.9 percent of applicants who are accepted. As the annual
cost for tuition, fees, and books is $55,750, you are forced to apply
for every loan and grant possible. It is a frightening thing to plunge
into this much debt, but you have faith that a high-paying job will
be yours upon graduation.

Exhausted from years of preparation, you sit in your first class
and think, "I've prepared so well that I won't need to take any notes.
I'll attend class and just remember what I hear and experience."

How wise do you think that would be? What do you think your
chance of success would be? Surely no one would work so hard to
be admitted to a prestigious university, pay an exorbitant amount
of money to be there, and then not take careful notes to review and
learn from.

Now, imagine another situation. In the premortal existence, a
tremendous spiritual battle was fought between the forces of good
and evil. You made the choice to fight for the forces of good and
to come to earth. Among the purposes of your earth life is to gain
a physical body, perform a foreordained mission, and to continually make progress toward perfection. An important way to make
progress is by gaining as much knowledge as you can. "Whatever
principle of intelligence we attain unto in this life, it will rise with us
in the resurrection" (D&C 130:18).

The Prophet Joseph Smith taught another motivating reason why
you should gain all the knowledge you can during your mortal experience. He said, "A man is saved no faster than he gets knowledge,

for if he does not get knowledge, he will be brought into captivity by some evil power in the other world, as evil spirits will have more knowledge, and consequently more power."[5] No wonder Heavenly Father wanted you to record your valuable lessons so you don't forget them.

Secular knowledge is increasing at a breathtaking pace. Not many years ago, I bought my first mobile phone. It was amazing to think that technology had reached a point where I could carry a wireless phone with me anywhere. Today, I carry another device in my pocket. It is a 2.5 x 5 x 0.25 inch marvel called a "smartphone" that houses almost every technological invention developed during the last century. It is a:

Telephone	Movie player
Computer	Voice recorder
Library	Typewriter
The Standard Works	Radio
Calculator	MP3 player
Flashlight	Navigation system
Still camera	Clock
HD movie camera	Day planner
Calendar	Newspaper
Game camera	Magazine
Movie editor	To-do list
Online shopping	Bank
Post office	Alarm clock
Search engine	Road map

It is almost beyond comprehension how quickly technological advances are being made. How is this explained? A simple answer is that brilliant research scientists conduct carefully planned experiments using the scientific method. Once they uncover knowledge, they meticulously record it and share that knowledge with the community. Businesses then take that knowledge and use it to make consumer products. New research experiments are then conducted, building on lessons learned from previous research. Each generation of researchers builds on the knowledge gained from the past, leading to continued progress.

Why then are individuals and families not making progress at the same rapid rate as technology? Why do so many retain the same weaknesses and make the same mistakes year after year? In fact, why are we as a society not making rapid forward progress. It seems we are actually regressing in areas like divorce, cohabitation, births out of wedlock, and crime? In theory, individuals and families should be making constant progress and each generation should be even better. Unfortunately, that is not the case.

How many of those who claim to understand God's plan for them are experimenting with ways to become more Christlike? And how many of them are recording the knowledge they gained for their own benefit and to eventually share with family and friends? It is no wonder that so few people are progressing to the point of finding real meaning in life or discovering the mission that they uniquely could perform. Perhaps the Lord would have us be more like a research scientist and "try the experiment to know if the seed was good" (Alma 32:36).

Prophets tell us to nurture the seed by recording our experiences and the lessons we learned. How can we know what the seed will grow into unless we try the experiment? And how can we have the faith to plant another seed if we do not record and remember past results? Too few are recording the grand lessons they have learned by experimenting with the Word. As a result, those lessons are buried six feet under, leaving the next generation to reinvent the wheel instead of building on past research.

How do we find information on making real progress in life? Some would say that by doing a Google search we can find any kind of knowledge we're looking for. For example, 0.21 seconds after typing the word "improvement" into the search box, 179,000,000 results pop up. Now that is impressive! If I read ten of those references a day, it would take me 49,041 years to see what is available at the present time on the topic of improvement. We can be inundated with so much information that we spend all our time "ever learning, and never able to come to the knowledge of the truth" (2 Timothy 3:7).

A far superior approach to gaining knowledge and making personal progress is to see what prophets have counseled us to do. Where do prophets get their information? Revelation is one way but certainly not the only way. Prophets have access to "researchers" worldwide. In the Church there are approximately thirty thousand bishops dealing with members every day. They see the results of experimenting on the Word—those following the teachings of Christ and those going directly against those teachings. These bishops share their research results with approximately three thousand stake presidents, who then share it with area authorities, who then pass it on to the Quorum of the Twelve and First Presidency. So when President Gordon B. Hinckley told the membership that pornography "only leads to misery, degradation, and regret,"[6] he based that counsel on "experiments" pouring in from all over the world. On the other hand, when you hear your leaders teach of the happiness that comes from following the teachings of Jesus Christ, you should listen because this research has also been conducted.

The Lord wants us to all to be research scientists when it comes to improving ourselves. This thought by Harvey Cluff comes across plain and simple: "No intelligent person in youth or old age should merely drift along. Look the world squarely in the face, listen and learn and not pass along, in life, indifferently, for there are grand lessons before you every minute."[7]

The key is to not only make personal progress but also to live a happy life, helping your posterity learn from the lessons you have learned. It takes time to recognize the grand lessons in your daily life and then use them to make every day meaningful, but you can begin by keeping one question in your heart each day, from the moment you wake up to the moment you close your eyes to sleep: What lesson can I learn from this? That is the first step, but it is not all. The Lord has commanded you to record what you have learned.

By attempting to make every day meaningful, do not limit your education to the classroom, talks, books, magazines, radio, or TV, though you will find lessons there. Every minute of your day can be spent in a "classroom" of your own making when you wake up excited to see what lessons you can learn, for yourself and for your posterity and those around you.

Upon the completion of this book, you will have the patterns you need to:

- Recall the experiences from your life that have taught you meaningful lessons.
- Record a meaningful experience in ten seconds and in a way that you never forget it.
- File your meaningful experiences in life by topic for quick access.
- Enjoy an endless supply of material for conversations, lessons, talks, books, or articles.

- Prepare talks, lessons, and articles in a fraction of the time.
- Easily write a multi-volume history of your life to leave for posterity.
- Greatly increase your knowledge and make better decisions.
- Feel increased gratitude for what you have been given.
- Realize the weaknesses holding you back and learn how to overcome them.
- Better understand why you feel the way you feel and act the way you act.
- Find more joy, happiness, and meaning in your daily life.

Notes

1. Oliver Huntington Autobiography, BYU–Special Collections, 26.

2. Joseph Smith, *History of The Church of Jesus Christ of Latter-day Saints*, edited by B. H. Roberts, 2d ed. rev., 7 vols. (Salt Lake City: The Church of Jesus Christ of Latter-day Saints, 1932–51), 2:198–99.

3. Journal of Wilford Woodruff, September 6, 1856.

4. Spencer W. Kimball, *The Teachings of Spencer W. Kimball*, ed. Edward L. Kimball (Salt Lake City: Bookcraft, 1982), 349.

5. Smith, *History of The Church*, 4:588.

6. "Excerpts from Recent Addresses of President Gordon B. Hinckley," *Ensign*, July 1997, 73.

7. Harvey Cluff Autobiography, typescript, BYU–S, 8.

CHAPTER 2

Seeing the Hand of the
Lord in Your Life

Wilford Woodruff: "We are the people ordained of God to establish His kingdom upon the earth, build up Zion, and prepare the way for the coming of Jesus Christ. Now, should we not keep a journal, record, and history of the dealings of God with [us] as they transpire day by day before our eyes? We should."[1]

While reading the biography of President Gordon B. Hinckley, I noticed that the Lord was preparing him for a great future work throughout his life. Even before he was called to be a General Authority, President Hinckley had important responsibilities working with the media and temples. In 1953, President David O. McKay had him find a way to present the temple instruction in various European languages. This was in preparation for the temple being built in Bern, Switzerland. After much study and prayer, President Hinckley recommended that the sacred ceremony be filmed in various languages. The film was first produced in English and then in seven additional languages. The Church now uses the film version in every temple in the world, except Salt Lake City and Manti.

When my wife and I were married in 1972, only fifteen temples were in operation worldwide. During President Hinckley's concluding address at the April 1998 General Conference, he mentioned that seventeen temples were then under construction, more temples than existed when we married. During this same talk, he surprised his listeners with the following: "I take this opportunity to announce to the entire Church a program to construct some thirty smaller temples immediately. They will be in Europe, in Asia, in Australia and Fiji, in Mexico and Central and South America and Africa, as well as in the United States and Canada. They will have all the necessary facilities to provide the ordinances of the Lord's house."[2] Again, looking back over this prophet's life, you can see the pattern emerging early on as the Lord prepared him to be the greatest temple builder in history. In all, he dedicated eighty-five temples in various countries throughout the world.

We can see the Lord's hand in the lives of our prophets because they keep records of their experiences. When they speak and write, they share those experiences as lessons learned. President Hinckley taught that record keeping is for everyone and promised many blessings to those who follow this counsel. In his gentle way, he said, "May I suggest that you write, that you keep journals, that you express your thoughts on paper. Writing is a great discipline. It is a tremendous educational effort. It will assist you in various ways, and you will bless the lives of many—your families and others—now and in the years to come, as you put on paper some of your experiences."[3]

It is not just prophets and apostles that have important missions on earth. Though your mission may not have you be the greatest temple builder in history, it will be something important and you will be required to give an account of your stewardship in the future. President Spencer W. Kimball taught, "Before we came here, faithful women were given certain assignments while faithful men were foreordained to certain priesthood tasks. While we do not now remember the particulars, this does not alter the glorious reality of what we once agreed to. You are accountable for those things which long ago were expected of you just as are those we sustain as prophets and apostles!"[4]

Journals Show You the Person You Have Become

If you fail to record the tender mercies of the Lord—along with the trials you face and your successes—it will be difficult to see the big picture of life as is expected of you. By reviewing your written records over time, the events of your life will come together to help you realize what mission the Lord has sent you to accomplish.

Consider the following journal entries made by Lori, one of my students at BYU in the early 1990s. She was struggling with the thought of nearing college graduation without a marriage prospect. Perhaps knowing she was most likely moving away from her heavily Mormon community to Washington, D.C., added to her concerns. Lori may also have wondered if the Lord was even aware of her and her fears. She wrote:

> Friday, February 14
> The day of love, what better day to remember the love of Christ. I dread Valentine's Day each year because first, I don't have a boyfriend to lavish gifts on me and second, because of the first, I feel like such a low rider. I thought this year that I would escape and forget Valentine's Day by going on this trip. I would concentrate on my job interviews and that is it. Well, I was wrong.
>
> As I awoke this morning, I hurriedly got ready to go to my first interview, which happened to be the most important one. I ate breakfast and began a small walking tour of the city. The first person I came across as I was entering the subway was an old man in rags. He greeted me with a "Happy Valentine's Day" and apologized for not having any candy or flowers for me. Quickly in my mind was the thought to keep on walking. My conscience would not let me, and I found myself stuffing a dollar bill in his can. Never have I seen such love and gratitude as was in this man's eyes. I hopped, skipped, and jumped onto the subway. I was ready for the interview.
>
> I approached the building to where my interview was and found two elderly ladies, whom I opened the door for. I walked into my interview with love in my heart and it must have radiated because the interview went well and they offered me the job I was dreaming about for months. . . . Where else could I have had such success and love than from the gospel of Jesus Christ and trying to become more like Christ?

In this journal entry, Lori exemplified the counsel of President Spencer W. Kimball: "Those who keep a personal journal are more likely to keep the Lord in remembrance in their daily lives."[5] She was feeling a little down and unloved on Valentine's Day and was given a tender mercy by a man in rags instead of a handsome prince. Perhaps this experience was part of the Lord's preparation for her special mission in life. If so, she will always have the memory in her journal to remind her that the Lord was aware of her at that crossroads in her life and sent people to help answer her prayers.

Here is another of Lori's journal entries from the next day, which gives us another glimpse of the Lord's involvement in her daily life.

She was still in Washington, D.C., and had been joined there by a BYU friend:

> Saturday, February 15
> This day I spent doing more of my favorite things: shopping! I also began to notice the blessings in my life.
>
> After a long day of shopping, we were headed to the Hard Rock Café to eat and bust our eardrums. The rain was coming down hard and we were running through town. As I passed some benches, I noticed there were boxes and boxes of garbage, or so I thought, that were covered with plastic. Later, I learned it was someone's home that was trying to keep the rain out. I thought of the analogy of "no time and always in a hurry" as I ran past these precious children of the Lord who needed my help! It is so heartbreaking because I think, what could I do to make their life easier? How could I have made a difference in their life?
>
> This incident reminded me of a trip my family took to New York City about ten years ago. We were on our way back to our hotel from a Broadway play and there was a blind man without legs sitting on the street. In the bustle, my family kept on walking. The man stuck in my mind and, when I got back to the hotel, I made my parents take me back to give him some money. We searched and searched but could never find him. I felt so bad that I cried all night. To this day, I still think about him and wonder what has become of him.

Based on this small glimpse into Lori's life, would you say that the Lord is preparing her for something special? Can you see a pattern? The experience in New York City when she was twelve years old made her very sensitive to those who are less fortunate. Ten years later, a man in rags made her Valentine's Day special. Then she sees the homeless under boxes as "precious children of the Lord who needed [her] help." I lost track of Lori and have no way of knowing what she is doing in her life, but I have a feeling that she is performing her earthly mission, wherever she lives.

We Are the Lord's Hands

Looking at the experiences of others can help you recognize that you need to look closer for the Lord's involvement in your own life. President Spencer W. Kimball said, "The Lord answers our prayers, but it is usually through another person that He meets our needs."[6] Throughout my life, people have been sent to help me when I prayed for help. During other humbling times, I know the Lord has expected me to be the answer to someone else's prayers. One of those experiences began in England a few years ago and is still unfolding today. It has been a testimony to me that the Lord is aware of me, has a hand in the experiences that I am offered, and knows that those experiences need to be recorded for me to see them in full perspective.

In May 2010, my wife, Wendy, and I traveled to England for speaking assignments in Preston and Durham. Our granddaughter, Dorothy, had served in the England Leeds Mission, returning home in November 2009. Knowing Durham was within her mission boundaries, I asked her if any missionaries she had served with were still in that area, hoping to meet one. She told me that Sister Crawford, her favorite companion, had been in that area but had finished her mission just three weeks earlier and returned home to northern Ireland.

We flew into Manchester on a Monday and were met at the airport by Elder and Sister Simonsen, medical missionaries from our Texas home area. We drove to the Preston Stake Center, next to the England Missionary Training Center and the Preston Temple. I was scheduled to speak to a group of young adults there. While I was setting up in the chapel, Wendy was in the foyer talking to Sister Simonsen about their mission. Knowing they were responsible for multiple missions throughout Europe, Wendy asked if they had crossed paths with Dorothy. The answer was no, but the Simonsens had met Sister Crawford. Less than five minutes later, a couple walked through the door and Sister Simonsen announced, "Hey, there is Sister Crawford!" As it turned out, Camilla Crawford had decided to return to spend several days in the Preston Temple, seeking guidance from the Lord for what her mission in life was to be. She had invited Darren, a friend from her home stake in Ireland, to come with her. As soon as they had pulled into the parking lot, someone had told them about the YSA fireside that would be starting a few minutes later. They walked in about ten minutes before the fireside began.

I was introduced to Camilla before the fireside started. My topic that night was, "Achieving Your Life Mission." The message seemed to resonate with her and, for the next three days, we attended several temple sessions with Camilla and Darren and took them out to eat. There was an instant bond with Camilla. We loved her from the moment we met her and could see why she was Dorothy's favorite companion. What are the odds of our meeting Camilla that night at a fireside about achieving life missions, when she was seeking inspiration on that very topic? It seemed more than a coincidence. We exchanged email addresses and kept in contact with her in the months that followed.

In March 2011, we received an email from Camilla asking if we would be in Salt Lake City the first weekend of April for general conference. She was coming to America to attend. Though we wouldn't be there that weekend, we were going to Utah to direct an EFY session the weekend after conference and Camilla would still be there. What are the odds that Camilla from Ireland and the Wrights from Texas would be coming to Utah at the same time? We had a wonderful time with Camilla and had some lengthy discussions about what her future held.

On Saturday afternoon, after our EFY training ended, we took Camilla with us to Provo to view an exhibit of paintings by Carl Bloch at the BYU Museum of Art and to walk around the campus. Camilla told us that she had been accepted to two universities in England and one in Ireland. I asked her about the institute programs near the schools. She told me there were few people her age that attended regularly. A feeling of concern entered my heart that if she attended one of those schools, she could be lost. I can't really explain what happened next but I suddenly felt like she was one of my own daughters and she needed help. I also felt that both she and her parents had been praying for answers and that I had a responsibility to counsel her with the information and expertise I had available to me. I had worked in the education field most of my life and knew how often young adults needed direction at that critical time of life.

I felt a prompting to ask her why she wasn't considering BYU. She laughed and said she had no desire to attend school in Utah. She voiced several mission stereotypes such as, "All Utahans take the Church for granted," and, "They live in an unrealistic bubble, far from what the world really is." These weren't the responses I expected after feeling inspired to ask the question. I challenged her to ignore the stereotypes and see for herself. She pointed out the stumbling blocks: she had no student visa, no money, no place to live, and no college entrance exams. She had not even applied to BYU and the deadline had passed. But she had already been accepted at universities in the United Kingdom. These were minor challenges that did not dissuade me from continuing my bombardment of encouragement for her to at least consider the possibility.

As my wife and Camilla were viewing Carl Bloch's paintings, I stepped out to call the BYU Admissions Office about a possible student from Ireland. They suggested she come to the office to talk about the requirements for a foreign student to be accepted. I said nothing to her about my call at that point.

Later, we walked into the Wilkinson Student Center. I said a quick silent prayer that Camilla would meet someone that would make her feel welcome and spark a desire to attend BYU. At that moment, I heard the answer to my prayer. "Brother Wright, what are you doing here?" It was John, a tall, handsome returned missionary from Georgetown, Texas, and a friend of our daughter Natalie. He was on campus to apply for the master's program in business administration. "John, this is Camilla Crawford from Belfast, Northern Ireland," I said. "She is going to come to school at BYU."

Camilla stared at me as John gave her a big bear hug and told her she was making the right decision. We talked for a while and by the time we parted, John and Camilla had a date set up for the following Monday night.

After we left, I confessed to Camilla that the folks at the BYU Admissions Office were expecting her. Afterward, Wendy and I flew home to Texas, and on Monday Camilla followed my advice and went to the Admissions Office and later on a date with John. I know what you are thinking. No, Camilla and John did not marry and live happily ever after. And no, she was not granted immediate admission to BYU that day. But she did have a date with a man who treated her better than any date she had before and gave her a hint of what she wanted in a husband. And she did receive solid advice from the Admissions Office on the educational path that would bring her to a Church school. What are the chances of John walking through that building at the exact moment that I needed him that night? I could not have prayed for anything more perfect than that "chance" meeting. Camilla returned home and, with her parents' blessing, came back to Utah to attend the LDS Business College in Salt Lake and obtained her associate degree just as the BYU counselors had suggested.

Wendy and I have enjoyed spending time with Camilla every time we visit Utah. On December 11, 2013, I received an email from

Camilla: "This week I am getting ready to move to Provo to start my new job at BYU . . . Heavenly Father knows exactly what we need. It is fun to remember just how stubborn I was in not wanting to go to BYU, how the Lord softened my heart, and how I've spent the last two years working my tail off to get there. I'm very grateful to John for taking me out on that date. He was a great gentleman. I've met lots of wonderful gentlemen here and I look forward to meeting some more at BYU—that are above the age of nineteen!" Camilla has a testimony that the Lord is involved in her life and she is recording her experiences to verify that.

Learning Things from Others

Some may wonder why I would take the time to record the Lord's hand in other people's lives. While helping me realize His involvement in my life, such stories inspire me in the same way that reading about other people's lives in the scriptures inspires me. If I don't record the experiences that confirm miracles are happening in my life and in the lives of those around me, those stories will be lost.

Orson Pratt elaborated on the importance of keeping written records,

> [If every person had] kept a faithful record of all that he had seen, heard, and felt of the goodness, wisdom, and power of God, the Church would now have been in the possession of many thousand volumes, containing much important and useful information. How many thousands have been miraculously healed in this Church, and yet no one has recorded the circumstances. Is this right? Should these miraculous manifestations of the power of God be forgotten and pass into oblivion? Should the knowledge of these things slumber in the hearts of those who witnessed them, and extend no further than their verbal reports will carry them? . . . We should keep a record because Jesus commanded it. We should keep a record because the same will benefit us and the generations of our children after us. We should keep a journal because it will furnish many important items for the general history of the church which would otherwise be lost.[7]

For example, because someone who was not even a member of my family kept a journal, I learned things about my paternal ancestors that I otherwise never would have known. While I was serving as president of our family association, we decided to apply to the state of Texas for a historical marker in honor of my great-grandparents William and Joissine Williamson. After our family received approval for the historical marker, we discussed what we could do for the dedication ceremony. In our family history chest, there was a copy of the Book of Mormon that the elders had given to my grandmother Epsie when she was baptized. In the back of it someone had written Elder Reed (Spanish Fork, Utah) and Elder Joseph Brooks (Mesa, Arizona). Arlen, a granddaughter of William and Joissine, was serving as our family historian at that time. She suggested I call the missionary department to find out more information on these two elders in the hopes that we might contact their descendants.

I called the missionary department but was told that they did not have any records on these former Texas missionaries. At our next family meeting, I informed the other officers of the dead end. I didn't feel like we had enough time or information to track down any descendants of these missionaries before the dedication of the marker. After several minutes passed, our historian, Arlen, said, "I feel I should write to the postmaster in Mesa, Arizona, to see if he knows anyone who lives in his area that may be a descendant of Joseph Brooks." I tried not to laugh at her suggestion to write to the postmaster of a large city and ask if he knew anyone with an ancestor who may have served as a Texas missionary for the Church more than a century ago. I thought she was wasting her stamp, but I didn't say anything.

A few weeks passed and our dedication ceremony was nearing. One day I received a call from Arlen. She said, "Guess what we got in the mail today?" The postmaster had received her letter asking about descendants of Elder Brooks. The postmaster had remembered an elderly woman named Mildred Jones whose maiden name had been Brooks. She had lived in Mesa but had since moved to California, or so he thought. The letter was forwarded from California and then to Phoenix, Arizona, where it finally ended up in the hands of Mildred Jones, the daughter of Joseph Brooks.

She wrote back to Arlen, congratulating our family on the historical marker and thanking us for the news that William and Joissine's descendants were doing well. Along with the letter, she included the personal missionary journals of her father from 1899 and 1900. It was a tender mercy from the Lord as I read the journals and found the following entries about my great-grandparents:

Mon., 8 Jan. 1900
The next day it had clouded up a little. We decided to go down in the lower part of the county and try to get through with it before it rained, as it was very low and swampy. We stopped all night with a widow by the name of Coffin.

Tues., 9 Jan. 1900
The lady we stopped with was quite wealthy. The post office was there. The place was called Weiss Bluff. We mailed our reports. It had rained some of the night before and it was very cloudy. The lady started us out on a road but we got lost. We could not see the sun so lost our direction but finally came out all right. We came to a place. The man's name was Williamson. He was a very nice old gentleman. This was about dinner time. We took dinner with him. He asked us if we would stop and preach for them that night. We had got a little out of our county but we told them that we would preach. We had a very good time.

Wed., 10 Jan. 1900
When we got up in the morning it was raining. It continued nearly all day and most of the night. At night, it slacked up a little. A few of the neighbors came in and we held a meeting at the same place. We stopped over night with the same man we did the night before with Mr. Williamson.

Thurs., 11 Jan. 1900
The next morning the weather had cleared up but it was so wet and muddy that we could not travel. We were in a low swampy country anyhow. We stopped all day and night with a son-in-law of Williamson's by the name of W. C. Baker.

Fri., 12 Jan. 1900
We decided to go on a ways further. Mr. Williamson said he was going up to his daughters. She lived on our road so he went along with us. But when we got there we found out a big marsh was so high that we could not cross. Mr. Williamson asked us to come back and stop over with him until after Sunday. We did so.

Sat., 13 Jan. 1900
We stayed with Mr. Williamson. Elder Reed was sick part of the day but was all right the next morning.

Sun., 14 Jan. 1900
The weather was then clear but it was very wet and muddy. It was Sunday. There was preaching there that day. The preacher wanted us

to take part with him. He was a freewill Baptist. We had a very good meeting. After meeting, we went back to Mr. Williamson's and stayed the remainder of the day and night.

Mon., 15 Jan. 1900

It had clouded up a little. We decided to get out of that part of the country before it rained any more. One of Mr. Williamson's sons said he would haul us across that big marsh. We were very thankful to him for his kindness to us. Otherwise, we would have had to wade it and that would have been very disagreeable. We left that settlement with some very earnest investigators.

My grandmother, Epsie, also wrote about the missionaries' visit:

Most everyone used tobacco in one form or another. Some of the children and many of the women smoked pipes and so not to antagonize the people and teach them slowly, they were taught just a few principles of the gospel at first. In one discussion with Uncle Billy's family, they made the remark, 'If you can find one thing by the Bible that we teach isn't true, we will leave the country. If we are not teaching the truth, we would be better off at home.' So they left promising to visit them again in the spring.

When the elders returned in April 1900, my great-grandparents were ready for them. They answered all of the family's questions and concerns. Great-grandfather William was sick at that time, so he was carried to his baptism in the back of a wagon. On the banks of the Neches River in Orange County, Texas, the elders helped William into the water and baptized him. Joissine was also baptized that day, and their daughter Epsie followed a short time later. William lived only seven months after his baptism, but all of his adult children soon followed his example and were baptized members of the Church. A Sunday School was organized later, then a branch. At this writing, there are four large wards in the area. At last count, the Williamsons have some 5,054 descendants. Almost all are members of the Church. I'm sure when Elders Reed and Brooks returned home from their missions, they had no idea the impact they had made on that corner of Texas. They helped prove that "by small and simple things are great things brought to pass" (Alma 37:6).

I'm grateful that Elder Brooks kept a journal of his experiences. I only wish he had recorded more about my ancestors and less about the weather, but even from that I can learn about the importance of details. I'm also grateful that our family historian acted on a prompting and, in doing so, taught the family that the hand of the Lord is involved in the details of our lives.

Notes

1. Journal of Wilford Woodruff, Feb. 12, 1862.

2. Gordon B. Hinckley, "New Temples to Provide 'Crowning Blessings' of the Gospel," *Ensign,* May 1998.

3. Gordon B. Hinckley, "If Thou Art Faithful," *Ensign*, Nov. 1984, 91.

4. Spencer W. Kimball, "The Role of Righteous Women," *Ensign*, Nov. 1979, 102.

5. Spencer W. Kimball, "President Kimball Speaks Out on Personal Journals," *The New Era*, December 1980, 27.

6. Spencer W. Kimball, "Small Acts of Service," *Ensign*, Dec. 1974, 5.

7. Orson Pratt, the *Millennial Star*, 11:153.

CHAPTER 3

The Necessity of Recording Family Stories

John A. Widstoe: "As I view it, in every family a record should be kept. . . . That record should be the first stone, if you choose, in the family altar. It should be a book known and used in the family circle; and when the child reaches maturity and gets out to make another household, one of the first things that the young couple should take along should be the records of their families, to be extended by them as life goes on. . . . Each one of us carries, individually, the responsibility of record keeping, and we should assume it."[1]

In 1999, I was called to serve as a counselor to President Kent Richards of the Texas San Antonio Mission. Upon hearing that he was a fifth-generation mission president, I wondered how it was possible that one family could produce a chain of five mission presidents in a row when there are so few called to serve.

Each of us has been raised in a family that is unique to others. No two families are exactly alike. All have distinct experiences that can teach family members valuable lessons, but only if they are shared. Unfortunately, far too few families share with their children and grandchildren their life experiences and lessons learned. When people know their family history and feel connected with the past, positive outcomes often follow. Dr. Marshall Duke, an award-winning psychology professor at Emory University, and his colleague Robyn Fivush studied the impact that family stories have on the adjustment and resilience of children. After years of research, Doctor

Duke concluded that children who know about their family background are more resilient than those who do not.

According to Dr. Duke, family stories "help children by evoking pride, personal history, a sense of connectedness and feelings of being special, even in the most ordinary family." He also said, "There are heroes in these stories, there are people who faced the worse and made it through. And this sense of continuity and relatedness to heroes seems to serve the purpose in kids of making them more resilient."[2]

The family of President Kent Richards has a close connection with the past. They admire and look up to their ancestors. The sharing of family stories has played a role in the remarkable legacy of the Richards family. Willard Richards, a physician, received a copy of the Book of Mormon near Boston, Massachusetts in 1835. After reading one page of the book, he said, "Either God or the devil has had a hand in that book, for man never wrote it!"[3] He read it through two times in ten days and was baptized in Kirtland in 1836 by his first cousin—Brigham Young. That decision led to a life of Church service.

Willard was one of the original missionaries sent to open Great Britain to the preaching of the gospel. He was Joseph Smith's private secretary and went voluntarily with the Prophet to Carthage Jail. Shortly before the mob stormed the jail, Joseph asked Willard if he would go with him into another room for safety. Willard's answer must thrill his many descendants. He replied, "Brother Joseph, you did not ask me to cross the river with you—you did not ask me to come to Carthage—you did not ask me to come to jail with you—and do you think I would forsake you now? But I will tell you what I will do; if you are condemned to be hung for treason, I will be hung in your stead, and you shall go free."[4]

While serving as Church Historian, Willard penned 1,884 pages related to the history of Joseph Smith. He was leader of a pioneer company that crossed the plains and later served as a counselor in the First Presidency to President Brigham Young. To say that Willard Richards served as a role model and hero for his descendants would surely be an understatement. Imagine the intense feelings that burn in the hearts of his posterity when they read this letter Willard wrote to Brigham Young and Heber C. Kimball while leading a group across the plains:

Sept. 10th 1848. Sweet Water River. About 334 miles east of Salt Lake City. I am here about the same as ever tho' not quite so big, yet I have not been dressed since you saw me, except in the big round about you saw, I have not sat up half a day at a time or rode only on my bed more than an hour or two at a time and that seldom. The induration of the liver is decreasing, but it is less than week since any one could discover I had any ribs. Loathsome bile, makes room for frequent vomitings and little food stays on my stomach, but enough of this. What do I want to trouble anybody with such personal affairs for? I don't. On the whole, or, in short I am pretty well, and if I can get over the mountains without another chill such as I got one year since, I may yet be quite well, but if not, and the marrow of the teeth [does not] go with the skin, it will be a miracle. Well, suppose it is we have had several miracles since we started[,] several children have been run over by loaded wagons & been healed almost immediately, and taken all together[.] Perhaps no Camp from Winter Quarters has ever been blest more than this division thus far, and when our teams appear used up, as tho' they never could start again a day or 2 or a week's rest recruits them, and we move again, and again, and are a-going to keep moving. Go ahead is my cry all the time, and when the cattle drop dead roll them out of the road, and go ahead.[5]

Willard was extremely sick when he wrote that letter and had been for some time. Yet he wrote, "I am pretty well." Surely these recorded stories, borrowing the words of Dr. Duke, "help children by evoking pride, personal history, a sense of connectedness and feelings of being special." Many of Willard's descendants have carried on the tradition their ancestor began when he said to keep moving and go ahead, no matter how difficult the situation appears to be.

Our Personal Heroes

Elder Carlos E. Asay expressed regret that our ancestors may become forgotten heroes and heroines. He said, "How sad it is when people fail to maintain records and write stories of themselves and loved ones. They allow great men and women to become known to their progenitors as just a name on a headstone, part of a vague memory recounted occasionally in family circles, or something less. Such negligence is an affront to heroes and heroines of the past, and such negligence denies blessings to the children of the present." [6]

Several of my ancestors have become my heroes and heroines since I read their words. For example, my great-great-grandmother Laura Geck Martin, along with her daughter Nelia and son-in-law

James Thompson (my great-grandparents), were baptized into the Church in 1897 in Alabama. Nelia wrote a brief life history in her later years, and my mother recorded several stories too. Like so many of her era, Nelia had very little formal education, but that didn't stop her from making her best effort at writing, and I treasure her style. Here she tells the story of their conversion:

> That fall we moved up near my mother's, so just before Christmas or sometime in the late fall, Elder Reed and Elder Burnette came to Mama's. So one evening here came Harman—that was her little boy—saying the new preachers had come and wanted us to come to preaching that night. My husband [James] jumped up and said, "Thank the Lord, I will hear what they have to say about the gospel." So we went. They were mighty fine men and knew how to preach too. And they preached the gospel in "a nutshell" and told all about it. So going home, that night he said, "Now, that's the way it's got to come and no other way, and if them men can prove to me what they said, that will be my church."

> So the next morning he went down to the river to a store where he traded. So when he got there, the elders were there. They and the grocery man were in a debate. His name was Stilling and he was a deacon of that church up there and a well-read man. So my husband just sat down on the counter and listened to them and they just "wound" old Stilling up so he couldn't say a word. It just did my husband so much good! When they got through he asked the elders to go home with him but they told him they were going some other place that evening but would be at his house the next day for dinner and would preach there that night. So that was the way it happened.

> But I'm here to tell you for I was in it all and when he began to investigate this gospel, it was made as plain as day to him—through his dreams and visions. He was not a well-read man but he had a good understanding and never forgot what he heard. Well, then after he made up his mind the gospel was true and he wanted to be baptized. But the elders never came through there very often at that time, so it was winter and I was in no shape to be baptized. But in February, they came back, Elder Reed and Burnette. So he, my mother and I were baptized on the 15th of February 1897 on a cold, rainy day and away down in an old pasture.

As I read that experience again for the umpteenth time, I am deeply touched by their willingness to accept the gospel and remain faithful under very difficult circumstances. I am proud to be one of their descendants, and their story creates in me a desire to live up to the high standards they set. I have always loved the faith-promoting stories of the pioneers who were willing to give up everything to cross the plains and come to the Salt Lake Valley. My ancestors chose instead to stay in the deep South and remain a faithful minority in the face of extreme prejudice. I picture my ancestors trying to live the principles of the gospel with no other members in the area. They had the Book of Mormon, a few other Church tracts, and occasional visits from missionaries, but there were no wards or branches to support them. Because they faced their trials and were faithful and determined, my grandchildren are now seventh-generation Latter-day Saints.

Nelia and James had a son, James Alvin Thompson, who was my grandfather. With no other Church members in the area, he married Ida Belle Seale, a faithful Baptist. Because they could not agree on which church to attend, they agreed to compromise and raise their children as Christians, but neither was to attempt to sway the children toward the Mormons or the Baptists. At forty-one, my grandmother Ida Belle gave birth to her ninth child in Mobile, Alabama. My mother, Mabel, wrote about that day in her journal years later.

The day was May 5, 1938, a day in my life never to be forgotten. A memory that will go with me to my grave. After all these years, I cannot look back on this day without tears flowing freely.

I can still see all us kids standing there on the dirt road in front of our house watching a car drive up—something we didn't see often for there were very few cars on the road in those days. It was my Dad, his oldest sister, Lilly Belle, and her husband, Grove Ikner. They were all crying. They had taken my Mama to the hospital before daylight that morning to have us another baby. It was now about 4 p.m. They brought news that both Mama and the baby were dead.

No one can really understand what those words meant unless you experienced it yourself! We were no doubt a pitiful sight. Both of my parents were forty-two years old then. My Dad was a small man, never weighing over 145 pounds, a share farmer who never had more than the bare necessities of life, although he worked so very hard.

Now he was left with four little kids, the oldest thirteen years old and the youngest not yet two. Who wouldn't cry! But crying was the easy part! What were we going to do?

I look back on this scenario today. Yes, it hurt, it hurt really bad. There aren't words to describe the hurt. Little did we know what lay ahead. Little did I know that my life would never be the same again.

All my life I had had my Mama. She had always been there for me. Never again would I have the privilege of living in a home with a mama and a dad. Never again would I have a mama that was there waiting when I came home from school. I could run and tell her what I did that day. Never would I have a mama that I could go to with my problems or answers to my many questions.

She loved to hear Arnold and me sing. It always made her so happy when we sang together. Now she would never be there to encourage us. Our Mama wouldn't be there to cook, to wash our clothes, to tell us bedtime stories, or to hear our prayers at night. We'd never again hear those precious words from her lips again, "I LOVE YOU!"

The list could go on and on and on. But, as hard as things got, life went on and somehow we managed.

Life is filled with many trials. This was a sad time for me. But when I look back, as hard as it was, I learned many valuable lessons that prepared me for the next five years. I realize now that I learned lessons that made me the person I am today.

Was this part of the plan for our family even before I was born?

Even at ninety years old, my mother would be reduced to tears when she talked about the loss of her own mother. She was reluctant to share a remarkable follow-up to the story, in part because when she was young someone had responded to her oral account with mockery and disbelief. I finally persuaded her to write it down, telling her it could help others dealing with the death of a loved one. Here it is in her words:

Grandmother Appears

After my Mama died, I could not be consoled. I cried for days. About five days after the funeral (which was in Uriah, Alabama), I was home alone. I had boils on my legs and bottom and they hurt really bad. We had what we called a bunk-bed. It was about the size of a single bed. It was in our front room and was used as a couch. I was laying on it on my stomach as I couldn't lay any other way nor could I sit down. I guess I more or less cried myself to sleep.

Whether I was asleep or awake, I do not know, but my Mama came to me, appearing very sad. She said she was heartbroken to see me like I was and wished I wouldn't cry so. She said she was in a beautiful place and could be very happy there if I could dry up my tears and go on with my life.

She also said that everybody who died had a chance to return to life if they wanted to, but nobody wanted to go back. She said it was wonderful where she was. Then she pleaded for me to try to be happy.

All my life, I'd seen my Mama sick, in pain, and worried. She'd had so many babies and had been told over and over not to get pregnant again. She no doubt had the fear that she would die. I had prayed hundreds of times for the Lord to make her well and not take her away.

Was this the answer to my prayers? Could I let her go so she could at last be happy? Maybe that's how I dried up my tears and accepted the fact that Mama was gone and that she would never come back. I came to a realization that I must accept this and go on with my life and do the best I could.

I never told anyone about this experience. I kept it to myself. I didn't figure anyone would believe me anyway. Finally, after a lot of years had gone by, one day I told someone, thinking they would surely believe me, but they didn't. It really hurt me a lot because of the way they acted and the things said to me.

So I went a lot more years before I mentioned it again. That's why I leave this story for my posterity. You can believe it or not. But, my Mama DID come to me. I heard her, and I will always be thankful for this experience. It made an impression on me that I will take to my grave.

What would my life have been without this experience? I certainly grew from it. I didn't grieve for my Mama anymore. I was willing to accept the fact that her mission in life was over. She had done what the Lord sent her to do. She had given nine babies the chance to come to earth and receive a body. Only four lived, but we have been blessed with lots of descendants for her. I have four children, twenty-one grandchildren, and over fifty great-grandchildren, with more to come. We all owe Mama a lot! We would not be here now if it hadn't been for her.

One day I hope to see my Mama again. Now I can tell her that I did go on with my life and have tried to always do my best. I am so thankful the Lord let her return to talk to me, for her counsel was needed so I could go on with life. So, believe me or not. It was real to me. She did come back to me for those special few minutes and, because she did, it changed my life.

My mother, Mabel, was thirteen years old at the time her mother, Ida Belle, died. There were three younger siblings who were eleven, nine, and three years old. My mother had no choice but to drop out of school to help take care of her younger siblings.

Her grandmother, Nelia, lived in another state but came several times to help her grieving son James and his four children. During these times, she was free to tell her grandchildren faith-promoting stories from her religious background—the stories that James could not tell them because of his pact with Ida Belle to raise their children without indoctrination in the LDS or Baptist faith. These stories not only converted my mother to the Church, but they also have helped me over the years. Here is one experience recorded by my mother that had a great impact on me at a time when my testimony of the gospel needed a boost:

Grandma [Nelia] loved the Lord! She was never ashamed of the gospel of Jesus Christ. She put her full trust in her Heavenly Father and went to Him often. I've heard her comment on many occasions that she'd had her prayers answered so quickly that she often felt the Lord was very nearby.

She loved to tell people about the gospel. I remember so well one night while she was at our house. Daddy had gone to Mobile to take his vegetables to market and when the men of the community took their vegetables, they'd be gone all night. That night, one of my friends, who was a year older than me, was spending the night with us. After supper, we were sitting around talking when out of the blue, Clara (Peavy) said, "Mrs. Thompson, you've been to Salt Lake City, why don't you tell us something about your church."

What an opportunity!! Nothing could have pleased Grandma more. And for the first time in my life, I heard the Joseph Smith story described in the most beautiful manner I've ever heard then or since. I don't know what Clara thought, but to me, it was an amazing story and I sat there just spellbound. It was true, I knew it was.

When she finished, I begged, "Grandma, tell it again and don't leave out a word." Well, she didn't tell it over again that night, but she told it over to me many times in my life and I loved it each time. And to this day, I never tire of the Joseph Smith story.

It wasn't long before she had the missionaries call on us. That was my first experience with the missionaries. They gave me the lessons and I thrilled with the gospel message from head to foot. I never doubted it in any way. I knew with all my heart it was true and I was baptized soon after. Daddy was already a member but had never taken time to tell me about the Church and I'd never been to a Mormon meeting.

So as I sat there thinking, I couldn't help but thank my Heavenly Father for giving me such a special grandma. I asked myself, "What would life have been like without her? What would I have done all those years, especially my teen years when I needed guidance so much, without her letters?" Every week, come what may, there was always a letter from Grandma. She didn't wait for us to write for she realized that these were trying times and that we needed her words of council and wisdom. I could never have done anything bad because I could never let her down. I knew she cared and I knew she loved me.

Those words from the past verify what Dr. Duke and his colleagues discovered about the sharing of family stories. Nelia became more than just a role model to her granddaughter; she became a hero and played a huge role in preparing my mother to face difficult challenges in her own life. Those written words also carry the continuity of the gospel tradition to my family and me.

Elder Theodore M. Burton taught, "Much of what we now regard as scripture was not anything more or less than men writing of their own spiritual experiences for the benefit of their posterity. These scriptures are family records. Therefore, as a people we ought to write of our own lives and our own experiences to form a sacred record for our descendants. We must provide for them the uplifting, faith-promoting strength that the ancient scriptures now give us."[7]

Another experience recorded about my great-grandmother Nelia has helped me stand up to pressure many times over the years. My mother recorded the story to the best of her memory:

> I'd give anything on earth if I had listened more carefully, written down, or could remember some of the many experiences of her life so my descendants could benefit as I have from them. I took it for granted. I'd heard so many times how they received the gospel, how she was baptized on a cold February day in the river before my Dad was born in April. How she, Grandpa, and her mother were persecuted in that little old farming town in Alabama. They suffered much for the gospel's sake. There are so many, many things that I don't remember. I realize more each day how important it is to keep a journal. But, there are a few [stories] that have made lasting impressions upon me that I'd like to pass on now.
>
> She said that a short time after she and Grandpa joined the Church, they moved to another little farming town, for Grandpa was a farmer. They had no nice chapel to hold church in, as we enjoy today. In fact, they had nothing except for a little magazine that came once a month, called the *Liahona*, and through this they kept in contact with the Church. Every now and then the missionaries would come through. You can see how hard it would be to grow in the gospel there. Not only that, but they were the only LDS family for miles.

It was customary in those days for the women to get together in the afternoons to visit with each other on their front porches. Each would dip snuff as they talked. They'd take a little piece of sweet gum stick, chew the end until it looked like a little brush, then stick that brush down into the snuff, put it into their mouths, and then spit off the porch when enough saliva had accumulated. It looked awfully nasty to Grandma, but all the women kept encouraging her. This was really a big decision for her being new in the community. She wanted so much to be accepted, so one evening she got her a little stick, made her brush, and took her first dip of snuff. It tasted terrible, but being so determined to be accepted, she didn't complain. On her way home that evening, she stopped by the mail box and there, inside, was her *Liahona*. Immediately her eyes fell to the words that seemed to jump out at her as if they'd been written just for her: "Any mother who would take the filth called snuff into her mouth and then kiss her darling baby is not worthy of being a mother." She went home, fell upon her knees and begged the Lord to forgive her. She never again partook of the filthy stuff called snuff!

When I picture my great-grandmother falling to her knees and begging the Lord for forgiveness, I have greater strength to stand up to peer pressure. Nelia was like Alma and the sons of Mosiah, who made mistakes but turned their lives around and became powerful forces for good. My goal is to try and be like her and quickly repent of the mistakes I make. As her descendant, I also feel a great desire to have the self-discipline and foresight to record important experiences that made my days meaningful and pass them on to my posterity, just as she did for me.

Finding Meaning through Forgiveness

Nelia had a sister, Lillian, who was also one of the most remarkable women I have ever met. She had the ability to make others around her be their best selves because she radiated righteousness. After living in the South, she moved to Utah in her later years to work in the Salt Lake Temple. I got to know her when I was a student at BYU and she was in her late eighties. She had joined the Church as a young girl and tried to live the gospel to the best of her ability. After marriage, she and her husband, Claude, moved to Tulsa, Oklahoma. The first branch of the Church there was organized in their home. Lillian and Claude had three sons. One son, Freddie, was killed at age nine when a horse kicked him in the stomach. Another son, Art, was killed at age twenty-six when he was hit by a car while helping someone, whose car had broken down on the side of the road.

Her only surviving son was William, whom they called Billy. This son was the source of much heartache for Lillian. He began drinking and getting into trouble at an early age. He became a professional boxer and lived a very hard life. He could never hold a steady job. At one point, he married and had a daughter, but his wife left him and he never saw either of them again. When Lillian was widowed and moved to Utah, Billy followed her there. For a time, he was incarcerated in the Utah State Penitentiary, and it was there that he began writing poetry. After his release, he lived in a small apartment near his mother. He died shortly after his mother, a lonely man who had chosen to live a life of alcoholism and sin, despite his mother's teachings and example. She pled with him, loved him, prayed for him, and cried over him. But it was all in vain during her lifetime.

Two of Billy's poems are among the family writings I treasure. They were found in his small apartment just after his death. The first was written to his little girl who had been taken away from him as a toddler by her mother, who couldn't forgive Billy for his drinking and other faults. The second was to his mother, as she was always there to love him and forgive him no matter how many faults he may have had.

I Remember You
by Billy Markham

It was a long time ago when I kissed you good-bye
Yes, I let you go, but I'll never know why.
You waved a farewell as you went through the door
And I never once dreamed that I'd see you no more.

Your sweet baby picture is all that I own
To remind me that maybe someday, you'll come home.
The little pink pillow that cradled your head
And your little rag that sat on your bed,
Have been carefully wrapped and placed softly away
Just waiting for you to come home someday.

How I miss your gay laughter and your sweet baby touch.
If I only had known that I'd miss you so much
Things might have been different in more ways than one.
I'm the person who knows what your leaving has done.

37

Your picture has faded, through the years it has worn
Like this rum-sodden heart that's all tattered and torn.
But I gaze at it still, with a tear in my eye
For it's all that I have to remember you by.

She Forgave Me All
by Billy Markham

I took the color of rose from her cheeks,
    I put the snow in her hair.
I took the sunshine out of her eyes,
    And I put those dark wrinkles there.

I took the laughter away from her lips,
    I caused her to falter and fall.
No burden of hers did I ever share,
    But she forgave me all.

I caused her so many heartaches and tears,
    Too many for me to recall.
I wouldn't hear when she cried out to me,
    But she still forgave me all.

Her love for me was real and sincere,
    Even when she knew I was wrong.
She was always there when I needed her,
    Because her love was so strong.

Now never again will she weep for me,
    The burden she bore was too much.
She faded away like the rose in her cheeks,
    And death brought the final touch.

Oh, many sleepless nights I have known,
    And the tears I have shed since that day.
When an angel came down and took her hand,
    And led my sweet mother away.

From somewhere in heaven she watches me now,
    And soon I may hear her sweet call.
And then she will hold me again in her arms,
    The one who forgave me all.

I learned from Aunt Lillian's life story and from Billy's poems that my duty as a parent is to love my children and forgive them, no matter how far they stray. There is always hope for a rebellious child, regardless of how long it may take. I also learned from her example that living the gospel makes people happy, despite the trials they face in life.

A few years ago my wife, Wendy, was doing family history research on my line and discovered that Billy's temple work had not been done. It was an honor to go through the temple for someone whose story I had come to know so well. I learned that day that not only did his mother forgive him but the Lord did also.

Notes

1. *Utah Genealogical and Historical Magazine*, July 1920, 100.

2. Judy Grover, "Raising Resilient Kids," *New Jersey Family*, Nov. 2013.

3. Claire Noall, *Intimate Disciple: A Portrait of Willard Richards* (Salt Lake City: University of Utah Press, 1957), 101.

4. The *Millennial Star*, Vol. 24, 472.

5. Willard Richards to Brigham Young and Heber C. Kimball, in Brigham Young, Office Files 1832–1878, reel 55, box 41, fd. 28.

6. Carlos E. Asay, *Family Pecan Trees* (Salt Lake City: Deseret Book, 1992), 123.

7. Theodore M. Burton, "The Inspiration of a Family Record," *Ensign*, Jan. 1977, 17.

CHAPTER 4
Learning Meaningful Lessons from Others

Douglas Adams: "Human beings, who are almost unique in having the ability to learn from the experience of others, are also remarkable for their apparent disinclination to do so."[1]

One of the reasons we fail to make our desired progress is that too often we have to experience things for ourselves. Anyone who learns only from his or her own experiences is unwise. While personal experience is certainly the best method to learn certain things, it can be a waste of time or even dangerous when learning other things. All of us have only a short time to live in mortality and we need to make the best of every waking hour. You do not have time to spend retesting things that have already been answered. For some things in life, there are simply no dress rehearsals. For example, I don't have to try drugs to learn that they are addictive. Others have made themselves guinea pigs and proved that fact for the rest of us. On a more positive note, I can watch general conference, calculate the average age of the speakers, and learn from their example that certain lifestyle choices lead to longevity.

There are grand lessons to make every day meaningful all the time. Every person you encounter can teach you if you are paying attention. The following are six valuable lessons I have learned from others.

Lesson One: Look at the Positive Side

I met Camden on the first day of an Especially for Youth session held at Illinois State University. We immediately clicked and he sent me an email a few weeks after he returned home, sharing an experience that taught me a valuable lesson. As you read his account of a "missionary moment," remember that Camden was fifteen at the time.

> I have a story I was able to tell my family when we went to Oklahoma a couple weeks ago. I was at a Silver Hawks game on the fourth of July. The Silver Hawks is a semi-professional baseball team in South Bend, Indiana. As we got into the fifth inning, I noticed a married couple in front of us. They seemed very happy and probably in their mid-fifties. I suddenly felt the Spirit very strongly.
>
> The Spirit had told me something I hadn't ever felt so strongly. I felt prompted to teach her about the gospel. I was very confused. I had no idea who these people were. I wasn't necessarily nervous, just hesitant.
>
> After a few more promptings, I turned to my dad and told him of the prompting I had. He was also confused. I told him I didn't know how to tell them. I said, "What do I say?" He said, "I don't know, it's your experience."
>
> I noticed her wedding ring and thought, *Okay, I'll ask about their marriage and ask if they are religious and then tie it back to them being able to be sealed for eternity.*
>
> So as we were exiting the stadium, I waited at the top. They got closer to the top and my heart started to beat so fast. They got there and I turned to the woman and said, "Excuse me, ma'am, can I have a moment of your time?" You wouldn't believe her answer. She looked at me straight in the eye, said "no," and left.
>
> For a moment I was dumbstruck. How on earth could she say that to me? As I left I told my dad what happened. But as I walked to the car, I smiled. I was so happy. I had prayed for so long to have a missionary experience. As big of a failure as it seemed I had been, I had the Spirit I was asking for! Even though in my prayers I asked for a missionary experience and I never fully had one, the Lord provided me with an experience that I will never forget. I learned that some people may not be receptive to the gospel; however, it is how we act on the Spirit that counts. I got to feel rejection and for some reason it made me that much more excited to serve a mission. I know I will be turned down many times, but I cannot wait to serve Christ. Brother Wright, I love this Church.

Camden taught me that I could view a negative experience with a positive attitude. He was wise enough to see this encounter as preparation for his future mission. A statement by Joseph Smith verifies that Camden is on to something: "Remember that 'it is a day of warning, and not a day of many words.' If they receive not your testimony in one place, flee to another, remembering to cast no reflections, nor throw out any bitter sayings. If you do your duty, it will be just as well with you, as though all men embraced the Gospel."[2]

Here are some important lessons I learned from Camden:

- Always try to find the positive side of any situation.
- The desired outcomes we seek may be different than our preconceived notions.
- If you do your duty and share the gospel, you have a reward whether they listen or not.
- Rejection does not have to be devastating if you learn lessons from it.
- The Spirit can help us feel joy and peace even during trying circumstances.

Lesson Two: Everyone Can Change and Be Better

A few years ago, I taught a series of parenting classes for members of our stake. During one of the classes, I related an experience I had as a member of a bishopric. Right before a fireside was scheduled to begin, several deacons—including one of my sons—were giggling and being irreverent. Before I could remind these young men to be reverent, Julie—one of our beehives sitting in front of the deacons—turned around and said, "You boys are so premature!" My son Spencer laughed and said, "It's immature, Julie, not premature." Julie responded, "Yeah, well, whatever. You are." My point to the parenting class that night was that children are going to do things that are "premature" because they have not yet reached maturity. I asked those in attendance if any of them remembered having done something "premature," like misleading their parents. I wanted to remind them that everyone makes mistakes, but also that past behavior does not always predict future accomplishment. Aaron, a successful pediatric dentist, shared an experience that perfectly illustrated my point. Here is his story:

> I was nearing the end of fourth grade, and our music teacher was trying to generate some interest with a presentation about the school band. It was then that I decided I wanted to play the clarinet. After spending a few days consistently harassing my mom, she agreed to

comply with my desire. My mom's initial hesitations were not only due to the inevitable squeaks she would have to endure as I learned to play, but also the monetary sacrifice that accompanied the decision. With a "practice agreement" in place, it was off to the music store. I happened to be intrigued by one of the more expensive clarinets. Forty-five minutes and over three hundred dollars later, we left with my clarinet and a bag full of maintenance supplies.

This enthusiasm lasted maybe a month. The thirty minutes per day of practice that was agreed upon felt more like three hours as I watched my siblings and friends congregate outside after school for the neighborhood sport of the day. I totally lost interest quickly and it was a continual struggle for my mom to get me to practice. I was athletic and decided that I was "too cool" for school band. However, my mom was not accepting my argument. I already had some experience in manipulating my mom's decisions in my favor, but she was not budging on this one.

We agreed that I would give it one year, and then the decision to quit or continue was up to me. The next couple of months were long and dreadful for both of us. Though I was becoming more talented with the clarinet, I was still less than enthusiastic about my great idea. During the first week of fifth grade, we were sent home with our class selection card. We were given the option of taking art or music. As I sat in class and watched my friends check the art box, I remembered the deal I had with my mom and reluctantly checked the music box. That night, I again pleaded with my mom, but to no avail. The class selection card was signed without further discussion. The next morning as I sat on the bus staring at this card, I realized I had made my check in pencil. To me, it was the decision that any child in my situation would have made. With the help of an eraser, I was officially registered for art.

Things were going great. Though I was not making much progress with my clarinet talent, my load felt a bit lighter. I would come home from school, toot my horn for thirty minutes and rush out the door to play with my friends. As the weeks passed, there was one thing that began to weigh heavily on my mind. The yearly and well-attended night assembly with a performance from the school orchestra was approaching quickly. How was I going to explain why I was not participating? What was I going to do? The night of "the big show," my dad left work early and we had a special family dinner. I then got dressed in the required slacks and shirt, grabbed my clarinet, and with the worst feeling, we headed for the school. As we walked into school, with my parents smiling, I received a few odd looks from other students.

My classmates were confused as to why I was dressed like the orchestra and carrying my clarinet case when clearly I was no longer a member of the band. I decided to leave my instrument in a closet as my parents and I socialized before the performance. As I walked them to their seat, my parents each gave me a hug and told me good luck. I had successfully navigated through many precarious situations in the past, but felt a little uneasy about my chances of success this particular night. As the performance began, I found myself onstage, out of place, and without a clue as to what I was going to do. I stood there with ears too big for my head, a large grin, and waved to my parents as I pretended to play my clarinet. As that part of the assembly ended, I quickly realized that I did not fool many people, most notably my parents and the band teacher. As I was walking offstage, I noticed my parents leaving their seats. As they approached in the hallway, I could see the disappointment, embarrassment, and anger in their eyes.

As I explained my deceit, my mother's eyes began to tear. As we left the school, there was silence in the car, which was finally broken by the sweet voice of my mom saying, "We love you" and a quiet chuckle from my dad. Unfortunately, that was not the end of my clarinet career. Due to my self-proclaimed wittiness, my mom made me do another year of school band. In addition, she enrolled me in weekly private lessons with her as my personal escort to ensure I was getting the experience I deserved. Needless to say, however, my clarinet career ended one year later.

Aaron made a mistake misleading his parents. He paid a price by having to endure another year of band and private clarinet lessons. However, his mistake did not prevent him from learning a lesson about deception. He went on to become a successful pediatric dentist, coach, husband, and father. All of us make plenty of mistakes in our lives. Some learn lessons from their mistakes and change while others continue to make the same mistakes over and over again. If you are to achieve a great mission in life, you need to learn to change and become better over time. American entrepreneur Jim Rohn said, "Your life does not get better by chance, it gets better by change."[3]

Here are the lessons I learned from Aaron's story:

- Everyone makes mistakes and everyone has the opportunity to change and be better.
- Kids making mistakes does not always predict future behavior.
- Wise parents impose consequences when their children intentionally mislead them.
- Parents should always let children know that they are loved, no matter what.

Lesson Three: Forgive and Forget

One of the most difficult challenges of life is forgiving someone who has treated you disrespectfully. President Gordon B. Hinckley testified of this fact and gave this counsel:

> How difficult it is for any of us to forgive those who have injured us. We are all prone to brood on the evil done us. That brooding becomes as a gnawing and destructive canker. Is there a virtue more in need of application in our time than the virtue of forgiving and forgetting? There are those who would look upon this as a sign of weakness. Is it? I submit that it takes neither strength nor intelligence to brood in anger over wrongs suffered, to go through life with a spirit of vindictiveness, to dissipate one's abilities in planning retribution. There is no peace in the nursing of a grudge. There is no happiness in living for the day when you can "get even."[4]

A student I had while teaching at BYU shared this journal entry about how he was treated on a much-anticipated date. He was an outstanding young man whom I had also worked with in the Especially for Youth program. I learned a great lesson from how he maturely handled a difficult situation.

Saturday, September 21

Tonight will be a night I will never forget. The day started off well. I worked at the MTC and had a really good experience with my missionaries. Then I went to work at the detail shop. While I was there I tried to figure out what I was going to do for my date tonight. It was a first date with a girl I have known since summer. We've done things together before but never as a formal date. I finally decided what I was going to do and I spent a couple of hours getting it ready. It wasn't going to be just a dinner and movies. I had planned what I considered to be my most creative date.

I was really excited both to see her and to carry out my plans. I thought that tonight was going to be the funniest date I have ever had. Boy, was I wrong. The whole night she was a brat. No matter what I did she wouldn't respond. It was as if she was determined not to have a good time. To make a long and very depressing story short, the night ended with her telling me how much of a jerk I am and how conceited and selfish and pig-headed I am. I had never had a date turn out like that. I was so angry I couldn't speak.

The only thing I wanted was to get rid of her. Then, all of a sudden I thought about the question: what would Jesus do? What bad timing! I had every right to be angry and even feel a little sorry for myself, but I couldn't. I don't know what it was exactly. I know that I never read a scripture that said that Jesus went out on a date, let alone go through the same experience, but I felt like Jesus wouldn't have reacted that way. For the first time, I felt justified in my anger. I had tried so hard to impress her and help her have a good time and she slammed me hard. But still, I couldn't be angry. Tonight I learned that forgiving and forgetting, even when they don't ask for it, is what Jesus would do. Oh well, so there's one less girl to go out with.

Tuesday, September 24

Guess what I did today? I put my pride in my back pocket and did something that my best friends thought I shouldn't have. Well, you remember about that date Saturday night? I realized that there's more to it than forgiving and forgetting and had to work through it. I realized that if I were to see her at school, I don't think we would talk to each other.

At first, I felt self-justified in that she was the mean one and I hadn't done anything wrong. In fact, I had even forgiven her without her asking. But that wasn't enough. I had to do something to make amends, even if she wasn't going to. So I got a rose and put a little joke on the card and sent it with a friend. I don't expect any reply; I am just content in feeling that I have done what Christ would have done had He been in my place. It's kind of hard to explain how I feel, but I picture Christ being made fun of and mocked and still He loved and served them. What happened to me was nothing compared to what happened to Him.

These are the lessons learned from Nathan:
- Not everyone will treat you with respect, even when you do kind things for him or her.
- You can still forgive people, even if they do not apologize for their behavior.
- Christ should be used as our example when we have questions about how to act.
- Things don't always turn out the way you imagined they would.
- We may never know the reasons behind a person's actions, so give them a break.

Lesson Four: Things Are Not Always as They Appear

As I supervised the early morning seminary programs in Austin, Texas, I heard this story from one of our teachers. It happened after one of her first days teaching seminary in her new home:

One afternoon I was home alone in the back bedroom of our new house. That day I had forgotten to lock the door and was surprised when I thought I heard the door open and someone enter the house. I could hear them rustling around so I slowly peeked out of my bedroom and was shocked to see a man that I didn't recognize inside my house. He had closed the front door behind him and was taking off his shoes. I had no idea who he was or what his intention was. He had obviously seen me looking out of my room because he started walking toward me. As he approached me, he stuck his hand out as if he wanted to shake hands with me. As I shook his hand, he informed me that he was there to make the repair I had requested on our new home.

It took me a little while, but I finally made sense of everything. At that time, I just started teaching early morning seminary at my house. The class began at 6:00 a.m. For the first couple of weeks I had put a note on the door for the students to read. After class, I would take it down and then put it up again the next morning. That day I had forgotten to take the sign down. The sign read:

- Don't knock
- Please come in
- Take your shoes off
- Come upstairs and shake my hand

I've always got a good chuckle out of that experience. I was impressed that the man would precisely follow those simple instructions he had read on the door and not question them. I have also thought how wonderful it would be if we were all as obedient to the teachings of the living prophets as the repairman was to mine that day.

These are the lessons learned from Joyce:
- Things may not be exactly what they appear to be.
- We need to be more obedient to the counsel given by the Lord's prophets and apostles.
- Make sure you always lock your door when you are home alone to avoid surprises.
- Share your humorous experiences with others so they can have a chuckle also.

Lesson Five: The Faith of a Child Is Powerful

During my time as director of the Austin Institute, I learned many valuable lessons from my students. One of the students I remember well was a married PhD student named Garrett. One day, he shared an experience in class related to the faith of a child. I asked him if he would write the story so others could learn from it. Here is what he wrote:

The winter of 2004–2005 was a difficult time for me personally. I was working nearly forty hours a week as a supervisor at the UPS facility in Belton, Texas, a job that was only supposed to be part-time. I traveled forty-three miles to work each morning. I usually woke up around 2:15 a.m. to be to work by 3:30 and normally worked until 9 a.m. Lately though, things were piling up and often I wasn't able to leave until 10:30 or 11 at the earliest. I would then rush to school at the University of Texas in Austin, where I was working on my PhD in Hispanic Literature. As a part of my degree program, I was also teaching a lower division Spanish class for the department. My days were long and my nights were short. I was finding it extremely difficult to do all that was required of me. I was not yet in despair and generally felt optimistic about everything though the line between the two was very thin and deep down I was struggling.

My oldest son, Kayson, had just turned seven and was beginning to enjoy sports, especially football. In a way, I think he was trying to connect with his dad whom he was seeing less and less of with every passing day. I helped coach his flag football team and almost instantly Kayson became a Texas Longhorns fan. It took a while for me to hop on the Longhorn bandwagon, but the spectacular play of quarterback Vince Young in the 2005 Rose Bowl soon won me over. Kayson had found his first hero that wasn't from a comic book. Near Valentine's Day, Kayson's first-grade class was given the assignment to make a valentine for someone special. I think the teacher intended for the students to make one for family or friends. Most made them for moms, dads, or grandparents, but Kayson didn't think like the rest of his classmates. He made a special valentine for his hero, Vince Young. When he showed it to me, I looked at the first-grade handwriting and drawing and praised him for his artistic ability. Then I said something like, "Wow, son, that's nice. I'm glad you are thinking of others."

Then Kayson said something that floored me. "I want you to take it to school and give it to him." I almost laughed out loud at the request and tried to explain that I didn't know Vince Young and had never seen him on campus. Kayson softly replied, "Just take it and give it to him, Dad." I again tried to explain that with over 50,000 students and faculty on campus at any given time. It wasn't very likely that I was going to see him, and I didn't have time to go all over campus and look for him. Kayson persisted, "Just take it, Dad. You'll see him and you can give it to him." Reluctantly, I said, "Okay, I'll do my best." Kayson's eyes lit up and he smiled and put his arms around me in a big hug. "I know you will, Dad. You'll see him." I wasn't looking forward to his disappointment when I didn't. The thought came to me that I could probably just take it to the campus sports information office or athletic department and they could give it to him, but I could just hear Kayson's words in my head: "Give it to him, Dad" and I knew that anything less than a personal encounter would bring certain disappointment. I sat the valentine on the counter, hoping he would just forget about it.

The next morning, as I was preparing to leave at 2:30, I turned on the kitchen light and the first thing I saw was the valentine. I knew what Kayson expected, so I carefully put it in my backpack and added an almost frivolous attachment to my morning prayer. "And, oh yes, Father in Heaven, if there is some possible way that I might run into Vince Young at school today, please let it be so. Thy will be done." Off to work I went, giving no more thought to the valentine or Vince Young at all. It was a rough day; I ended up doing the job of a sick employee and had to stay late to get my own work done. By the time I got to the school, I only had about thirty minutes to shower, change, and get to class on time.

That day, as I pulled up to the building, I saw three or four big, athletic-looking young men walking by in UT burnt orange and surmised immediately that they were football players. The valentine flashed in my mind and I looked at them intently to see if maybe Vince was one of them. Sure enough, he was there, walking right by my car. I called his name and beckoned him over to my car and, laughingly, popped the trunk and pulled the valentine out of my backpack and told him that my son was one of his biggest fans and had made the valentine for him. I sheepishly and nervously laughed as I gave it to him and he smiled when he heard the story. I urged him to keep it, but he asked if I had a pen, signed it and gave it back and told me to tell Kayson to keep playing football and to do well in school. He walked away and I never saw him again, except in the limelight of television where he propelled himself to stardom and NFL glory. In the next season, he became the Heisman Trophy runner-up and led the Longhorns to another Rose Bowl victory and a national championship.

I immediately called my wife and she agreed to tell Kayson that I had a surprise for him when I got home. After telling him the story, I gave him back the valentine. He just smiled and said, "I knew you would," and ran off to play. My wife saved it and made a special page for it in Kayson's scrapbook. It was a special day for us both.

These are the lessons I learned from Kayson:

- Our goal should be to have the faith of a little child if we want miracles to happen.

- We should keep our children's special mementos so they will have them later.
- If you teach children to have faith in prayer, they will believe you.
- We should realize that the Lord really is involved in our lives in intimate ways.

Lesson Six: In Negotiations, Use a Win-Win Approach

As I sat writing this chapter, I received an email from our daughter Nichelle, who lives in Utah. She shared a Christmas request letter written by her eight-year-old daughter, Madison. See if you can learn some of things I did from reading this letter.

Dear Mom and Dad,

I deserve A Dog Seat pet, A unicorn tummy stuffer and a rainbow loom for three resons. Reson number one. I work hard in school. For example, I got all A's on my report card. Reson number two I am kind to evreone. For example, I let Riley [sister] and Hunter [brother] keep my Toys without giving me somthing. Reson number three, I will let anyone be my friend. For example, when Alex asked to be my friend I said yes. Now I know I already have alot of toys But here are three things That will hapen if you get me all Three presnts. First if you get me The tummy stuffer I'll get Beter grades, Second if you get me the seat pet I'll do Better on my tests, last if you get me the rainbow loom I'll make new friends by giving bracelets I make from the rainbow loom. That is why I deserve Those presnts for crismas! love Madison fort

These are the lessons I learned from Madison:
- Little children are a lot smarter than some give them credit for.
- Parents better be on their toes if they don't want to get outsmarted by their children.
- It always good in negotiations to strive for a win-win situation for both parties.

Elder Richard G. Scott said,

I will share a principle that, if understood and consistently applied, will bring enormous blessings throughout your life. It is not difficult for me to explain, nor for you to understand. However, it will require of you significant, determined effort to yield its full potential. With it you can learn vital truths that will bring you greater, enduring happiness and make your life more productive and meaningful.[5]

Notes

1. Douglas Adams, *Last Chance to See* (New York City: Ballantine Books, 1992).

2. Smith, *History of The Church*, 1:468.

3. Jim Rohn, *7 Keys to Freedom* (Bloomington, IN: Balboa Press, 2013), 113.

4. Gordon B. Hinckley, "Of You It Is Required to Forgive," *Ensign*, Nov. 1980, 62.

5. Richard G. Scott, "To Acquire Knowledge and the Strength to Use It Wisely," BYU Devotional, Jan. 23, 2001.

CHAPTER 5

How to Use Your Grand Lessons

Spencer W. Kimball: "As we read the stories of great men, we discover that they did not become famous overnight nor were they born professionals or skilled craftsmen. The story of how they became what they are may be helpful to us all."[1]

One reason so many people neglect to make a record of the important events of their lives is they don't understand how useful those lessons can be. Here are seven ways that I have found recorded lessons helpful in making every day in my life meaningful:

1. Personal Growth

A main benefit of keeping written records is the personal growth that can come by doing so. President Hugh B. Brown taught, "It is incumbent upon us, therefore, to encourage and keep alive the questing spirit, to learn and continue to learn everything possible about ourselves, our fellowmen, our universe, and our God."[2] A questing spirit is one that is seeking or pursuing something. Every day should be an expedition to discover as much as you can. Asking the question, "What lesson can I learn from this?" can turn a simple experience into a valuable lesson. By preserving the details in writing, personal growth can occur. Here is my journal entry of a lesson learned from my sons:

Boys' Lemonade Stand

Nathan, who is six, and his brother, Nolan, who is four, decided to open a lemonade stand for a day with two of their cousins in front of our home. It was an extremely hot and humid Texas day and I felt sorry for them as they stood patiently waiting for their first customer. Time dragged on and the chance for turning a profit looked bleak. With sweat pouring off their faces, they continued to wait for someone to come. But no one did. I couldn't take it anymore, so I drove to their "Pa Pa's," who lived down the street and explained their plight to him. A businessman himself, my father was very sensitive to his aspiring grandson's situation. He told me he would come over right away and buy some lemonade.

A short time later, he pulled into our driveway right beside the lemonade stand. The kids were very excited as he was their very first customer of the day. The boys were very pleased when he ordered four glasses of lemonade from them. As he waited for his order to be filled, Nathan said, "Pa Pa, you are going to have to move your truck out of our driveway?" A little surprised, he asked, "Why, do I need to move?" Nathan continued, "Because we're expecting a lot of business here any minute."

In reality, there was no rush of business to the lemonade stand even after my father moved his truck. The boys did have a couple of customers come from across the street, but that was it. They were a little disappointed after having their hopes of getting rich dashed but they were not discouraged. Most of us have had multiple experiences when our ideas don't work out the way we had hoped and planned. After experiencing a few failures, many begin to look at life with pessimistic lens and lose hope that "a lot of business will be here any minute."

So was the lemonade stand really a failure? Not at all, if viewed with the proper lens! Some choose to keep a positive attitude through ventures that appear to be failures and learn lessons and improve. Unfortunately, many fail to learn lessons from their lemonade stands and consider them failures and wastes of time because there was no clear gain. Perhaps the reason you don't see many successful pessimists is because they are convinced that nothing they try will work, so they never try. They let their lemonade stand experiences of the past kill any desire to take risks in the future. If you are to be successful in life, it will not happen by sitting around and never trying anything. Remember that every brilliant idea that you have will fail a hundred percent of the time you never try them. Why not try those you feel strongly about to see if they will work? There is, of course, a possibility that your ideas will not work out exactly the way you had hoped. If that is the case, it is imperative to ask why they did not work and learn lessons from the experiences.

I learned many lessons that day, which have proven meaningful over the years. The boys taught me that it always helps to have a positive attitude when you are sweating and things look bleak. What appears at first to be a total flop, may turn into a success if we learn from the experience. One thing is certain: there is a hundred percent chance of failure if you never try your ideas. Last, I learned that trying to sell ten-cent products in a low traffic area is not a good business model.

2. Teach Your Children

A precious teaching moment occurs when children ask you to tell them a story from when you were their age. If you don't seize these opportunities, your children may quit asking. There is something powerful about using personal experiences to teach lessons. All too often parents draw a blank when asked to tell a story from their past. If experiences from your life are recorded, you will not miss those valuable moments.

When our five children were younger, they loved hearing stories from my childhood. They especially liked to hear them at bedtime. But because I was not always available at bedtime, I made audio recordings of several stories. The children listened to them over and over when I was away. Here is one of their favorites:

Brian Snapping Turtle

As a child, I always looked forward to summertime when we visited our cousins who lived out of state. I loved it when my Uncle Jim and his family visited from St. Anthony, Idaho. My cousin Brian and I always had a great time together. One summer, we went exploring and found a snapping turtle. Brian had never seen a turtle like this before. How do boys play with a snapping turtle? They poke a stick in the vicinity of the turtle's open mouth trying to get it to bite the stick.

This turtle had powerful jaws and snapped onto the end of the stick. The turtle took the bait several times, snapping the end off of the stick each time. When Brian tired of this game, he decided to pick up the turtle with his hands. That day, Brian and I both learned a couple of valuable lessons about snapping turtles.

We discovered that turtles' necks are much longer than we thought. If the turtle is being poked with a stick, its neck extends out only as far as necessary to snap at the stick. But in reality, a turtle can stretch its neck almost halfway across its back. We also learned that turtles can strike with unexpected speed, like a snake. Brian learned all of this firsthand, so to speak. When he picked up the turtle, its long neck extended out and the turtle's powerful jaws clamped onto Brian's finger like a vice.

He started yelling for me to get it off of him, but I had no idea how to do that. Brian raised his hand up in the air, but the turtle gripped even tighter. In severe pain, Brian tried a helicopter spin over his head and finally flung the turtle off. Bleeding and crying, but with finger still intact, Brian was nevertheless a lucky boy as adult turtles have been known to bite off fingers and toes. Brian still has a scar on his finger.

At this point in an account, I like to add the "moral of the story" for my children:

> A lot of "snapping turtles" will tempt you to play with them throughout your life. I'm not talking about little snapping reptiles. I am talking about alcohol, drugs, cigarettes, smokeless tobacco, pornography, and immorality. You may think you can play with these kinds of things and not get hurt, but that is not true. Just when you begin to think you are having fun with them, they will reach up and grab you. You cannot play with temptation without getting hurt.

Teaching children can be a real challenge. That seems to be especially true when they are teenagers. Our prophets teach youth that they should not drink, use profanity, wear immodest clothing, listen to inappropriate music, watch R-rated movies, date before the age of sixteen, steady date, or date those who don't share their standards. When our youth go to school, however, they are often taught the opposite of these principles. To make things even more challenging for a concerned parent, other parents may not emphasize the same behavior standard. The time comes in the life of every child when he or she questions parental rules. Responding with, "Because I said so" is tempting but ineffective.

Using experiences from your past that taught you lessons can be just the thing you need to teach your children. My children are all married now and have children of their own. My bedtime stories are reaching a new generation, and one of the favorites is still Brian and the snapping turtle.

3. Reminiscing with Family and Friends

Few things bring extended family and friends closer than reminiscing about experiences from the past. At family gatherings, I love to hear, "Remember the time when . . ." As soon as someone begins a story, the memories of that incident come flooding into the minds of those involved and laughter often follows. Most families have classic stories that are told over and over again. Here is one that our daughter-in-law Kristi had when she was ten years old. Though I'm sure it was not funny at the time, you can imagine the laughter it brings as her family remembers.

911 Moon Boots

When I was ten years old, I woke up to one of those rare and glorious mornings in Boise when school was cancelled due to snow. I knew it was going to be a good day. Shortly after the cancellation was announced, I could tell my mom was flustered to have my sister and me home all day. She explained all of the errands she absolutely had to run, so I quickly chimed in that it was not a problem for me to stay home because I could invite a few friends over. My mom mulled this over and eventually caved and let me have my friends over to play.

Around lunchtime, several of my friends arrived at my house. This is also when my mom announced to us that she had to leave; however, we were not to leave the house. My mom then ordered my older sister to make sure us ten-year-olds would follow these vital directions. Little did she know . . .

My mom soon left and I immediately ran upstairs to my closet to show off my new purple "moon boots" [astronaut-inspired snow boots that are now a relic of that era]. We discussed the beauty of the moon boots for a while until someone had a great idea to put these moon boots to work and go sledding! It was a snow day, after all. I felt nervous about leaving the house since we had been firmly told not to, but it was hard to resist taking a spin in those cute purple moon boots. It seemed such a waste of moon boots not to go sledding on our snow day.

We left the house and walked about a mile down the road, dragging our plastic sleds behind us to the elementary school. I remember running up and sledding down those hills so many times with my friends. It was easy to lose track of time. It must have been a couple of hours before I actually realized I was tired, freezing, and that the cold had seeped into my boots. We finally started our trek home and I specifically remember listening to the sound of the sleds dragging loudly behind us over the snow and thinking, *Is it bad if I can't feel my toes?*

The minute I walked in my front door, I ripped those moon boots off and ran for my room. My friends followed close behind and I shared my secret that my feet were completely numb. My friend Brianne, whose mother was a nurse, immediately diagnosed me with frostbite. I was terrified. I thought, *Don't they have to amputate frostbitten feet and toes?* Brianne dragged me to the bathroom and plunged my feet into cold water, which instantly made me cry and my feet itch all at once. Then she picked up the phone and dialed 911. As I rocked myself back and forth, I could hear her explaining to the operator that I had severe frostbite and asking, "What should we do?" After only a minute, she hung up the phone. "They are on their way," she told me, which made me cry and itch my feet even more. I am not sure how much time passed as I swayed and itched, but soon I could hear the ambulance arrive at my house, followed by two police cars, which were then followed by a fire truck. Below, I could hear the various emergency people walking in and out of my house before I met an EMT. He looked at my feet for maybe a second before declaring I would survive this frostbite incident. Brianne bravely asked him why there was a fire truck in front of the house. The EMT explained it is standard procedure to send an ambulance, a fire truck, and two police cars to every 911 phone call made. I thought I was going to be sick.

And then my mom walked into our house and I knew I was going to be sick. Initially, she was terrified for my sister, worried about our health and safety and me. However, as people started trickling out of the house, her worry soon turned into anger. How could we have disobeyed her? I will never forget the feeling of being so terrified for my feet, so guilty over having disobeyed my mom, and yet so relieved that my mom was home and I was able to keep my toes.

Look back in your own memory for experiences you've shared with family members. Once an incident is remembered, summarize it in a three-word title to kick-start your memory of what happened. The next time you are with the relative, ask if they remember too. It will help you feel closer to that person as you share those memories.

4. Use Your Stories in Talks and Lessons

I have given speeches and conducted workshops in most of the United States, and a few foreign countries. Often I have had to squeeze a number of speaking assignments into a short period of time. In the summer of 2012, I spoke at EFY, the LDS Dental Association's annual meeting, BYU Campus Education Week, and at the Family History Center in Riverton, Utah, during a nineteen-day stretch. I gave a total of twenty-six talks on twenty-six subjects, with most of the talks being fifty-five minutes in length. The total time spent speaking was approximately twenty-two hours—the equivalent of giving 132 sacrament meeting talks in less than three weeks.

I was grateful that I had recorded thousands of personal experiences during my lifetime. I would not have been able to keep up that pace without my cache of stories and lessons learned.

President Thomas S. Monson uses personal experiences and the lessons learned from them frequently in his talks. Many people attribute his ability to recall specific details to a photographic memory. But he does not credit an unusual memory. He credits his habit of keeping a daily journal: "My daily journal, kept over all these years, has helped provide some specifics which I most likely would not otherwise be able to recount."[3]

Here is an experience President Monson recorded and then used in one of his classic addresses given to the Primary organization.

One day as we [the Primary] left the chapel for our classrooms, I noted that our Primary president remained behind. I paused and observed her. She sat all alone on the front row of the benches, took out her handkerchief, and began to weep. I walked up to her and said, "Sister Georgell, don't cry."

She said, "I'm sad."

I responded, "What's the matter?"

She said, "I can't control the Trail Builders. Will you help me?"

Of course I answered, "Yes."

She said, "Oh, that would be wonderful, Tommy, if you would." . . .

The years flew by. When Melissa Georgell was in her nineties, she lived in a nursing facility in the northwest part of Salt Lake City. One year just before Christmas, I determined to visit my beloved Primary president. . . .

I found her in the lunch room. She was staring at her plate of food, teasing it with the fork she held in her aged hand. Not a bite did she eat. As I spoke to her, my words were met by a benign but blank stare. I gently took her fork from her and began to feed her, talking all the time I did so about her service to boys and girls as a Primary worker and the joy which was mine to have later served as her bishop. You know, there wasn't even a glimmer of recognition, far less a spoken word. Two other residents of the nursing home gazed at me with puzzled expressions. At last they spoke, saying, "She doesn't know anyone—even her own family. She hasn't said a word for a long, long time."

Luncheon ended. My one-sided conversation wound down. I stood to leave. I held her frail hand in mine and gazed into her wrinkled but beautiful countenance and said, "God bless you, Melissa, and merry Christmas."

Without warning, she spoke the words, "I know you. You're Tommy Monson, my Primary boy. How I love you."[4]

When President Monson relates his inspiring stories, I am motivated to be better. I also am motivated to follow his example of recording the experiences that teach me lessons. Some may say, "If I ever had any dramatic experiences like President Monson, I would write them down, but I don't." Often what at first may seem simple and inconsequential can be so much more if pondered.

Consider an experience that President Dieter F. Uchtdorf used as a theme in a powerful general conference talk:

> Not long ago I was skiing with my 12-year-old grandson. We were enjoying our time together when I hit an icy spot and ended up making a glorious crash landing on a steep slope.
>
> I tried every trick to stand up, but I couldn't—I had fallen, and I couldn't get up. . . .
>
> That was when my grandson came to my side. I told him what had happened, but he didn't seem very interested in my explanations of why I couldn't get up. He looked me in the eyes, reached out, took my hand, and in a firm tone said, "Opa, you can do it now!"
>
> Instantly, I stood.
>
> What had seemed impossible only a moment before immediately became a reality because a 12-year-old boy reached out to me and said, "You can do it now!" To me, it was an infusion of confidence, enthusiasm, and strength.
>
> Brethren, there may be times in our lives when rising up and continuing on may seem beyond our own ability. . . . Even when we think we cannot rise up, there is still hope. And sometimes we just need someone to look us in the eyes, take our hand, and say, "You can do it now!"[5]

President Uchtdorf took a simple experience and, with thought and prayer, made it the theme of a powerful talk on doing what may seem impossible. That ordinary act of falling on the ski slope helped to plant the message of the talk much deeper into the hearts of those who heard it.

5. Help in Your Occupation

If you were asked to name the most successful figures in technology within the last thirty years, who would they be? Names such as

Michael Dell, Steve Jobs, Mark Zuckerberg, and Bill Gates would come likely to mind. Can you name the one thing that these men all have in common? It is not an MBA from the Harvard Business School; none of the four have college degrees even though business schools throughout the nation use their ideas in classes. One thing we know about all of them is that they were not born with the knowledge they possess. We also know that they didn't learn how to be a success in the business world in a college classroom. They learned in non-traditional ways and used that knowledge to reach the pinnacle of business success.

During one of my last classes at BYU, a professor shared a humorous anecdote to teach critical-thinking skills. Our assignment was to figure out what was happening before having all of the facts revealed. See if you can figure out what happened before you know the full story.

Train Loud Sound

During World War II, a general and his aide, a lieutenant, were traveling from one base to another. They were forced to travel with civilians aboard a passenger train. They found their compartment where two women who were already seated—an attractive young lady and her unattractive grandmother. For most of the trip, they conversed freely. The train entered a long and very dark tunnel. Once inside the tunnel, the passengers in this particular car heard two distinct sounds: the first was the smack of a kiss; the second was the loud sound of a slap.

Though these four people were in the same compartment aboard the passenger train, they came to four differing perspectives. The young lady thought how glad she was that the young lieutenant got up the courage to kiss her, but she was somewhat disappointed at her grandmother for slapping him for doing it. The general thought to himself how proud he was of his young lieutenant for being enterprising enough to find this opportunity to kiss the attractive young lady but was flabbergasted that she slapped him instead of the lieutenant. The grandmother was flabbergasted to think that the young lieutenant would have the gall to kiss her granddaughter, but was proud of her granddaughter for slapping him for doing it. And the young lieutenant was trying to hold back laughter, for he found the perfect opportunity to kiss an attractive young girl and slap his superior officer all at the same time!

Had I thought more deeply about what the story meant when I heard it in my class, it might have helped me in a situation I found myself in shortly after graduation:

3M Copier Service

When I graduated from BYU, I worked for the 3M Company in their business products division. One day, I received a call from the office manager of a government agency who was furious with our service department. She had called for service on a 3M duplicating machine on two occasions and no one had ever come to service their copier. I was in sales and obviously wanted to keep the customer happy so I quickly went to visit her. She showed me the notes of the days she called and whom she had talked to. She had all the right numbers and all the right names, so I knew she was telling me the truth. When I saw her records, I too became upset with the service department and expressed that frustration to my immediate supervisor.

He wanted to talk to the disgruntled customer and get the full story before going to the service department. I thought we should go straight to the service department and tell them to quit goofing off and take better care of our customers. On the way over, I continued to badmouth our service department. My supervisor told me to remember that there are always two sides to a story. I thought he had a little too much company loyalty and needed to be a little more realistic. When we got to the office, the office manager was angry because of the problems caused by not having a photocopy machine. She again pulled out her records to document her calls and the IBM people to whom she complained.

At that point, my supervisor called our service department and asked them to explain why they had not responded to the two calls. He listened patiently as the real story began to unfold. It seems that when the woman called the first time, our service manager immediately called her supervisor and reminded him that their maintenance contract had expired and that they would be charged with a service call. He was asked if he wanted to renew this service agreement, but the supervisor said no. He never told his office manager that he was the one who canceled the call. When she called the second time, our service department called her boss again and they were again told not to come. And again, the supervisor never told the office manager what had happened.

That day, I was reminded that things are not always as they appear. I had wrongly vented my frustration about our service department without attempting to get to the bottom of the matter. My more experienced boss said, "There are always two sides to a story." We should withhold judgment until we have all the facts. This one lesson has helped me on multiple occasions, not only in my occupation but also in Church callings and in life in general. While most of us will never have the opportunity to run a multibillion-dollar corporation, we can learn and record grand lessons that will help us be more successful in our occupations.

6. Dealing with Adversity and Failure

President Ezra T. Benson once shared this profound thought: "It is not on the pinnacle of success and ease where men and women grow most. It is often down in the valley of heartache and disappointment and reverses where men and women grow."[6] If we are to accomplish our missions in life, we need to learn lessons from our successes as well as our failures. The following is an experience that taught me several grand lessons.

Texas Barbecue Festival

Years ago, I served on the board of directors for the Chamber of Commerce in the city where we lived. Our president challenged us to think of traditions that could unify our city. Even though I was extremely busy at the time, I spent hours learning what other communities did to create unity. Many had yearly festivals based around food like strawberries, crawfish, tamales, crabs, potatoes, salsa, chili, and so on. I thought it rather strange that no city in Texas had a festival based around barbecue.

I authored a proposal for an event called the "The Texas Bar-B-Q Festival" that included a cook-off, fun runs, beauty contests, carnival rides, food and craft booths, bands, dance groups, skydivers, and an outdoor concert. When I presented the proposal to the board, the idea was quickly approved. I was a little excited when they appointed me chairman. The excitement waned when I was told the Chamber had no money for the event. As I walked away, the festival didn't seem like such a good idea, but I felt obligated to try to pull it off.

A simple logo was designed at our kitchen table. Next, a fundraiser was scheduled to get things rolling. Taking a huge risk, we booked a country music star for the outdoor concert to be held in our football stadium. I had no idea what would happen if we didn't sell enough tickets to cover the cost involved but was relieved and hopeful when local newspapers and radio stations began giving us free publicity. Many got excited and several people volunteered to be in charge of different aspects of the festival. I spent hundreds of hours on the event myself in addition to the long hours at my regular job. Excitement was in the air as the anticipated date arrived.

The Thursday night opening went well. It appeared our first year would be a big success. I came home pretty happy! Shortly after I retired that night, a lightning and thunder storm rolled in, followed by heavy rain. I couldn't sleep. My stress level increased with each hour of rainfall. By Friday morning, widespread flooding was reported, with much the same predicted for the coming hours. At 9:00 a.m., the Chamber called an emergency meeting to make a decision on the concert scheduled for that evening. If we canceled, we were still obligated to pay the band half of the contracted price. If we didn't cancel and it was rained out, we would owe the full amount. Looking out on the flooded streets, we felt the only choice was to cancel the concert.

Late that afternoon, the rains stopped. Walking through the soggy festival site, I saw many damaged booths and disheartened participants. It is hard to describe how sick I felt. I went from being a successful legend in my own mind to feeling like a complete failure. I knew we (meaning I) had a huge concert bill to pay since all of the ticket money would need to be refunded. That night, I lay on my bed so frustrated, exhausted, and embarrassed that I cried. Why had I spent hundreds of hours planning and working on this event only to fail miserably?

The next day, the weather couldn't have been better and the scheduled events took place without a hitch. With money from booth rentals and carnival rides, we only ended up losing a little over $1,200—a huge relief. Knowing that we didn't ever have a budget for the event, I personally paid the money back. I have learned if I ever lose money trying something that it helps me to pretend it was just a tuition payment toward a business degree from the university of life.

Last year on a Saturday, we drove back to that area to visit my mother. I was shocked to see the familiar logo that I designed on a highway billboard, inviting all to attend the 30th anniversary of the annual Texas Bar-B-Q Festival that weekend. There were similar signs all over the city. I heard that country singer Clint Black had performed before a large crowd the night before. The festival included a queen, carnival rides, food and craft booths, multiple bands throughout the three-day event, and a huge cook-off. What started off as a miserable failure has now turned into an annual tradition.

Life has a way of humbling you when you begin to get proud. Most of us want instant success, but life usually does not work that way. I discovered that the lessons learned from failure in one area often help you grow in others. Usually, if you give your best effort, something good will come out of it. Finally, that experience taught me things that appear to be total failures might turn out to be successes in the long run.

7. To Use in Writing

At some point it occurred to me that the books I enjoyed reading usually had something in common: they included personal experiences to make their points. Perhaps that is why I often use personal experiences that taught me lessons to emphasize points in book chapters, magazine articles, and blog posts. The following illustrates this in the first book I wrote:

Several years ago my brother Jack bought a go-cart for his sons for Christmas. He lives in a neighborhood that has approximately thirty children under the age of sixteen, so you can imagine the excitement the go-cart produced. Every time one of the boys would get on to take a ride, about fifteen other kids would be running behind, begging for a turn.

After Jack, my father, and I observed the scene for a short time, we found a solution to the problem of who should get the next turn. In a nearby open field, we marked off a circular go-cart track. We then told the kids to get in a line and wait their turn for a ride around the oval track. My brother helped each new rider settle into the go-cart and then pushed it to get a fast start while my father and I enjoyed watching.

Everything was going fine until Jack's son Shay, age six, got on for his turn. He was excited, grinning from ear to ear. When he was situated on the cart, Jack asked him if he was ready to go. He answered by pushing the gas pedal all the way down and taking off. The neighborhood kids roared their approval as the tires spun on his quick start.

The track we had marked off was circular, but as Shay neared the first curve, he didn't turn when he was expected to and went straight instead. The children cheered even louder, thinking this was really exciting. But three adults were viewing the same scene in terror, for Shay was headed straight toward a major highway. Seeing the danger his son was in, Jack took off as fast as he could, sprinting after the speeding vehicle.

Just before Shay reached the highway, he turned the wheels and headed back toward the track. This allowed Jack to cut his lead and come within a few feet of the go-cart. But the chase was still on, as the father tried desperately to catch his speeding son. Then, as suddenly as it had begun, the chase was over. As Shay glanced triumphantly at his friends, the cart ran head-on into a tree. On impact, Shay's head went forward, slamming his mouth and nose into the steering wheel. Jack was running so fast behind him that he couldn't stop and crashed into the back of the go-cart, banging both legs at shin level.

By this time, the crowd had settled down and there was no longer excitement in the air as the battered go-cart rested against the tree and a bloody six-year-old walked toward us with his badly limping father.

I've reflected a lot about that experience and have since concluded that it is not unlike the situation in some of our families. How many parents do essentially the same thing with their children that my brother did with his? Like the go-cart ride, we spend little or no time instructing and training our children on how to navigate safely through the perilous journey of youth. Many teenagers embark upon their dating years about the way Shay did on his go-cart ride, grinning from ear to ear, but unprepared for the dangers facing them. When dangers do come, many of their peers, like Shay's neighbors, cheer them on through peer pressure. When parents finally realize the tremendous risks their children are facing, they often go chasing after them. Unfortunately, many times both the youth and the parents end up seriously hurt. Occasionally, one of the young people even ventures out onto a spiritual highway and is hit. Others are seriously injured, and some are even lost. In many cases, they could have been saved if parents had only trained and prepared them better while they were young, for the ride they would one day take.[7]

There are plenty of reasons to record the experiences that have taught you lessons. If you do, I promise that you will find multiple ways to use them in your everyday life.

Notes

1. Spencer W. Kimball, *The Teachings of Spencer W. Kimball*, ed. Edward L. Kimball (Salt Lake City: Bookcraft, 1982), 351.

2. Hugh B. Brown, in Conference Report, Apr. 1968, 101.

3. Thomas S. Monson, "Consider the Blessings," *Ensign*, Nov. 2012, 86.

4. Thomas S. Monson, "Primary Days," *Ensign*, Apr. 1994.

5. Dieter F. Uchtdorf, "You Can Do It Now," *Ensign*, Nov. 2013, 55.

6. Ezra Taft Benson, in Conference Report, Stockholm Sweden Area Conference, 1974, 70.

7. Randal Wright, *Families in Danger: Protecting Your Family in an X-Rated World* (Salt Lake City: Deseret Book, 1988), 2–3.

CHAPTER 6
Three-Word Summaries to Scripture Verses

Bruce R. McConkie: "Perhaps the perfect pattern in presenting faith-promoting stories is to teach what is found in the scriptures and then to put a seal of living reality upon it by telling a similar and equivalent thing that has happened in our dispensation and to our people and—most ideally—to us as individuals."[1]

The standard works contain God's wisdom and can provide solutions to the problems you face. When combined with your own experiences, the scriptures can be personalized to your circumstances and applied to a variety of settings. Typically, those who are regular scripture readers can turn to verses for timeless answers to today's questions. Nephi taught a valuable lesson when he said, "I did liken all scriptures unto us, that it might be for our profit and learning" (1 Nephi 19:23). I have learned to liken the scriptures to my own life. This has definitely turned out to be for my profit and learning. By doing this, we become another witness to the truth and applicability of those timeless words.

Jesus Christ taught about the need for extra witnesses to testify of truth: "But if he will not hear thee, then take with thee one or two more, that in the mouth of two or three witnesses every word may be established" (Matthew 18:16). The Bible is its own first witness and you become the second when you link its principles to your own experiences. So turn one of your personal experiences or observations into a three-word summary using a person, place, or thing to distinguish it from all other experiences. These three words will fit neatly into the margins of your scriptures next to a verse that teaches the same principle. When you see the three-word reminder, it will "liken" that scripture to you each time you read it.

For example, my Bible contains the three-word summary "Sinai You Qualify" in the margins of Exodus 16. In the summer of 1998, my wife and I were scheduled to take a guided tour of the Middle East, which included a stop in Egypt. However, in November 1997, a tragedy occurred at the ancient temple near Luxor. Six terrorists dressed as policemen killed sixty-three people, including fifty-nine foreign tourists. Many countries issued travel warnings to avoid Egypt and tour companies worldwide wrote the country out of their itineraries, including ours. The already-precarious Egyptian economy was devastated by the loss of tourism and its government scrambled to assure travelers that they would be safe there.

Right before we were scheduled to begin our tour, we got word that the safety of our group had been guaranteed by the Egyptian government and we would be flying to Cairo after all. The emotions in our group ran from excitement to fear. When we landed at the Cairo airport and walked into the terminal, we saw armed guards lining the walls. My first thought was that there had been more trouble and the troops had been called out to secure the airport. As it turned out, the men were our private army, assigned by the government to protect our tour group. We felt like foreign dignitaries on official business.

As we left the airport, a police car—with red lights flashing—escorted our two tour buses to a five-star hotel, the nicest I've ever stayed in before or since. We enjoyed huge buffets for breakfast and supper. Our room overlooked the city and the beautiful Nile River. Cairo, with its museums, antiquities, pyramids, and sixteen million residents, was the most fascinating city I had ever visited. Even the weather was surprisingly pleasant. In three short days, we grew to love the people and the city.

Egypt's minister of tourism hosted us at a banquet and delivered a speech that was broadcast on national TV. The food and entertainment were incomparable that night. As we quickly learned, we were the first American tour group to venture into Egypt since the terrorist attack, so our hosts used us to show the world that it was safe to return. I grew accustomed to being treated like royalty and didn't want to relinquish the throne.

When the time came to leave Cairo, we continued by bus to Mount Sinai, located in a harsh desert. No longer did we have armed guards, buffets, trees, or rivers. There were no stunning pyramids in sight. In the late evening, we pulled up to a half-star motel at the base of Mount Sinai. They offered us a buffet dinner that looked as if it had been prepared several days before. I passed on dinner that night, leaving it to the flies that were swarming around the buffet table. When we were shown to our rooms, we found the beds hard, the pillows lumpy, and the shower leaky. I thought of Moses bringing the complaining children of Israel into the same wilderness. I kind of knew how they felt.

That evening, we regrouped outside for what was billed as a "very short" meeting with our leader in preparation for our two in the morning climb to the summit of Mount Sinai. The meeting was held in an open area with no chairs. There was no grass so we elected to stand rather than sit in the dirt. Several Bedouin children gathered around us, begging for candy and gifts. In the distance, we saw men riding camels.

Our tour guide opened the meeting with a primer on Old Testament history, and it soon became obvious that our meeting would not be short. The speaker was oblivious to the fact that we were tiredly standing in the dirt and in just a few hours we were to climb a mountain. Most of us were getting restless and many began mumbling negative remarks to each other. I was convinced our leader was going to rehash the entire Old Testament from Genesis to Malachi. Here we were in this forsaken desert within a few hours of beginning a difficult mountain climb. The situation was like night and day from Cairo and I found myself wishing we were back there.

As my discomfort escalated, two words popped into my mind: you qualify. Qualify for what? Then the little voice said, "You qualify. You could have easily been one of the murmuring children of Israel with Moses in the wilderness of Sinai." Like them, I wanted to go back to Cairo. Here I was, about to enjoy an unforgettable spiritual experience climbing the mountain where it is believed God gave Moses the Ten Commandments and all I could do was complain about the accommodations.

This is what that incident looks like in my scriptures.

Exodus 16:2–3

Sinai	And the whole congregation of the children of Israel murmured against Moses and Aaron in the wilderness:
You	And the children of Israel said unto them, Would to God we had died by the hand of the Lord in the
Qualify	land of Egypt, when we sat by the flesh pots [cooking pots], and when we did eat bread to the full; for ye have brought us forth into this wilderness, to kill this whole assembly with hunger.

Now whenever I read those Bible verses, I think about that night at the base of Mount Sinai. I understand what the children of Israel were saying to Moses, who was serving as their "tour guide" in the wilderness. As my memory of Sinai comes flooding back, I can imagine the verses in my own words:

Exodus 16:2–3

Sinai	And the whole congregation of our tour group murmured against our leader and his wife in the wilderness because of a long meeting.
You	
Qualify	And the children of the tour group said unto each other, would to God we had died by the hand of the Lord in the land of Cairo when we stayed in a five-star luxury hotel overlooking the Nile and sat by the all-you-can-eat buffet, and did eat six kinds of delicious meats and a huge variety of vegetables, breads, and desserts to the full; for our tour leaders have brought us forth into this wilderness, to kill this whole assembled group with half-star motels, stale buffets, and very long meetings.

By putting your own three-word summaries beside scripture verses that teach similar principles, the scriptures come alive as you read, and you become a witness of the principles and doctrines being taught.

Name Church Steeple

In the margin of my Doctrine and Covenants, section 1 (next to verse 3), I have written "Name Church Steeple." When I was a boy, there was a new LDS church built about a block from where I lived. One day, several of my friends and I went to the construction site to look around. One of the projects for that day was to pour the cement for the base of the new steeple. After the cement workers left, only my friends and I and the wet cement remained behind. "What could it hurt since it's going to be covered by the steeple anyway?" The decision was made that day to write our names in the wet cement. At that point in life, I had not learned the lesson that Elder Henry D. Moyle taught: "Our decisions, once executed, can never be erased."[2]

Shortly, the names of Marshall, Randal, Glen, and others were carefully preserved. I also put the year under my name. Several days later, the workers came back and finished erecting the steeple. It was exciting to look down the road and see the steeple and to know that as long as it stood, our names would lie hidden underneath. Later, I got a closer view of the new steeple and was shocked. The base of the steeple was shaped differently from what we had imagined. We had assumed the steeple would cover the entire concrete foundation, but we were wrong. All four corners were left uncovered. Now, with the steeple completely finished, Marshall's name was clearly visible on the left side next to the main sidewalk going into the chapel and on the right side was "Randal Wright 1963." All of the other names were covered up, but ours were there for everyone to see.

We got plenty of comments about our impulsive decision from both adults and the other youth in the neighborhood, but there was no going back. And as we quickly found out, sand paper and wire brushes are powerless to erase letters deeply etched in concrete.

Years passed and I grew up, married, and moved away to attend college. I had no idea at the time I had immortalized my name in concrete that I would move back to that very area with my wife and children. One day, our oldest son, who was nine, came home from Cub Scouts and said, "Hey, Dad, your name is in the steeple at the church." I quickly tried to change the subject, but it didn't work. My mind went back to the day we made the decision to write our names in the cement and how cool we thought it would be in the future. Now that I was a father, it wasn't nearly as cool as I had expected. "How did it get there, Dad?"

"Well, son, sometimes youth are just so outstanding that the adults want to do something in their honor." When he appeared to believe my joke, I decided that I had to come clean and explain how we had made a decision without thinking. I told him that sometimes bad decisions don't go away and that he needed to think things out before acting.

The steeple base has now been exposed to the elements for five decades, and yet I can still see our names. I am reminded of that choice we made long ago every time I visit my mother and brother, who still attend church in that building. What may seem like small decisions, made on impulse, can linger with us for years or perhaps for a lifetime.

Do you know of someone who has ruined a good name or jeopardized a life mission by bad decisions? We see star athletes who have lost everything by their decision to use performance-enhancing drugs. We see politicians who have destroyed both their marriages and careers by their decisions to have an affair. We read of the terrible consequences of those who made the decision to drink and drive. We see people in wheelchairs who were unfettered until they said to their friends, "Hey, everyone, watch this!"

Many have not learned the lesson that the Reverend Joel Hawes taught many years ago: "He that cannot decidedly say, No, when tempted to evil, is on the highway to ruin."[3]

Michael Cioppa also had it right when he said, "It's in your moments of decision that your destiny is shaped."[4]

Throughout history, lives have been shattered by single bad decisions often made in a split second. In the Old Testament, we read that David made a fateful decision to send messengers to have Bathsheba come to him. He proved that, before acting on impulse, it is wise to study it out thoroughly in your mind and then ask if it is the right thing to do. If you have an uneasy feeling after thinking it through, it is a sign that you should reconsider.

Doctrine & Covenants 1:3	
Name	And the rebellious shall be pierced with much sorrow; for their iniquities shall be spoken upon the housetops, and their secret acts shall be revealed.
Church	
Steeple	

My impetuous friends and I never foresaw the day when (then) Elder Thomas S. Monson would walk past that etched concrete when he came to dedicate that building in one of his first assignments as an apostle. I never thought I would receive a picture from a son-in-law who took some of our grandchildren to see the steeple and have them pose beside my youthful indiscretion. Our act has certainly been spoken of in the housetops and our secret has definitely been revealed.

James Seminary Primary

The third chapter of First Nephi in my Book of Mormon has these three words in the margin: James Seminary Primary. These words always remind me of this story:

I knew when I asked James to be an early morning seminary teacher that it would be a difficult assignment. As an employee in his father-in-law's sign business, he had a heavy workload. His children were also involved in a group that performed in various areas, requiring him to be out of town frequently. It is not easy to teach a class of teenagers that begins at 6:00 a.m. five days a week, but James's priesthood leaders felt he was the one the Lord wanted for the assignment. He told me all of the reasons he didn't think he could accept. Having taught early morning seminary myself while working about fifty hours a week and serving on the stake high council, I could definitely empathize.

I told him to think about it and to let me know what he had decided. The next day he called and told me he would be happy to teach. I was a little shocked and wondered what had happened to change his mind. He said he and his wife were talking about our conversation and both had agreed that he was far too busy and probably should decline. While they were having the conversation about seminary, his wife's parents stopped by for a visit and James shared his dilemma. His in-laws were active Church members and James respected their opinions. After some discussion, all agreed that seminary would be impossible for him at that time. While they were talking about all the reasons James could not teach seminary, eight-year-old James Jr. walked in. After listening to the conversation for a moment, young James interrupted, "In Primary, my teacher taught us about Nephi. Nephi said he would go and do what the Lord said even when it was hard." There was silence in the room. After a long pause, everyone agreed that James Sr. should call and tell me he would be happy to teach seminary. That year he did a great job with the Lord's help.

1 Nephi 3:7

James

Seminary

Primary

And it came to pass that I, Nephi, said unto my father: I will go and do the things which the Lord hath commanded, for I know that the Lord giveth no commandments unto the children of men, save he shall prepare a way for them that they may accomplish the thing which he commandeth them.

John Movie Respect

I spoke at a youth conference in a Midwestern state about the influence of electronic media. As part of the talk, I quoted a statement by Elder Gene R. Cook. He said,

> I am not surprised that President Benson would counsel us, as members of the Church, to avoid . . . R-rated movies. Yet there are still many who are going to R-rated movies. I guess they have not really believed the President of the Church, and that is risky business. To me, some of the PG and PG-13 movies are even questionable. I have had some adults say to me, "Well, I'm an adult. I can see an R-rated movie. Of course I don't let my children see them, but I do." The scriptures tell us to become like little children, and we ought not to go where we can't take our children. If it's not good enough for your children, it's not good enough for you. We ought not to have double standards. There is one standard and it's the Lord's standard and we ought to abide by it whether we're old or young.[5]

After the talk, a young man named John, about sixteen years old, approached me. He was wearing the youth conference T-shirt and his build suggested he was an athlete. I could also tell that he was an outstanding example of a Latter-day Saint youth. When we were in private, he told me that he had a Sunday School teacher who had had a great influence in his life. He said that one Sunday she read a statement to the class from President Ezra Taft Benson who said, "We counsel you . . . not to pollute your minds with such degrading matter, for the mind through which this filth passes is never the same afterwards. Don't see R-rated movies or vulgar videos or participate in any entertainment that is immoral, suggestive, or pornographic."[6] She then challenged the class to make a vow to never see an R-rated movie. This young man said, "Because I loved and respected this teacher so much, I made a vow that day that I would never watch one of these movies."

He then told me that several months passed by. One Sunday, the teacher came in and told the class about a movie she had just seen based on the tragic events of the Holocaust. The teacher went on to tell them how good the movie was and pointed out the things that she had learned from it. One of the class members raised her hand and asked if this movie was R-rated. The teacher replied that it was but it was okay to see because it was based on history. Another student said that he thought someone had told him that there was nudity in the movie. The teacher sheepishly said that there was but it was not sexual. Then the young athlete said something that I don't think I will ever forget. He said, "I still love my teacher but I don't respect her." In a world with so few appropriate role models, it seems imperative that parents set a good example for their youth. N. Eldon Tanner said, "Improper parental example in the home is a leading cause of the wandering of youth from the principles as taught in the gospel of Jesus Christ."[7]

Jacob 2:35

John

Movie

Respect

Behold, ye have done greater iniquities than the Lamanites, our brethren. Ye have broken the hearts of your tender wives, and lost the confidence of your children, because of your bad examples before them; and the sobbings of their hearts ascend up to God against you. And because of the strictness of the word of God, which cometh down against you, many hearts died, pierced with deep wounds.

Bradford 200 Copies

In a discussion of the law of concentration in a Sunday School class, someone expressed that it would be very difficult to live the law because of all they would have to give up. I have heard that opinion expressed on many occasions over the years. I'm not sure where we ever got the idea that the law of consecration would lead to poverty. In the Book of Mormon, we read about a group of people who lived the law after the Savior's visit to the Americas. They were not poor, but "had become exceedingly rich" (4 Nephi 1:23).

Seldom do we speak about the benefits of living the law. As we were talking about this in the Sunday School class, my mind went back to a class I had at Brigham Young University.

My professor, Reed Bradford, was a gifted storyteller and emphasized those stories that taught valuable lessons. At the beginning of an introductory sociology class, he gave us an assignment that brought a round of complaints from the class. We were told to find a story that taught a valuable moral principle and summarize it in at least two pages, but no more than four. That was the easy part. The grumbling began when Professor Bradford told us to make two hundred copies of the story and bring them to class. Did he think we were made out of money? Even though there was an uproar among the students about the assignment, he did not back down. On the day the stories were due, we all came in carrying stacks of paper. It had been an expensive assignment but no one wanted to lose the grade points. When class began our professor pointed to a student in the front row and told him to take his stories and put them in the hallway on the floor along the wall. He then told everyone else to follow row by row. One by one, we went out and put our stacks down both sides of the hallway.

As we returned to our seats, I suspected that Professor Bradford would keep the stories to give away at his own pleasure. I even took a little comfort imagining how much time it would take him to cart all of those copies to his office. At the end of the class period, he said, "Now go back out in the hall and take one copy from each pile." As I took one story from each of the stacks, it finally dawned on me that there were approximately two hundred students in that class. Each one of us had come with one story and left that day with two hundred. I put forth very little effort and gained so much. That turned out to be a significant day in my life—the beginning of a huge collection of stories that have enriched my life and my work.

As with the law of consecration, everyone does his or her part and becomes "rich" in the process. The early Saints in this dispensation were unable to live the law in part because people were thinking of what they would lose. We have a modern correlation. In our day we pay our tithing and we get the use of beautiful facilities and enriching programs that we could never afford on our own, but some do not pay tithing because they fear to part with what they have. I once observed the building of a beautiful new Protestant church in our area and learned that the members had tried to raise the total cost of $1.5 million. They eventually raised $400,000 and had to borrow the rest from the bank. When Mormons pay tithing, the results are astounding. We have beautiful chapels and temples across the world. Chapels in poor neighborhoods are the same design as those in affluent neighborhoods. Living the law of concentration would bring even greater prosperity to members instead of taking it away. Sharing with others usually brings greater prosperity instead of less; however, that is not the reason we share.

4 Nephi 1:3

Bradford

200

Copies

And they had all things common among them; therefore there were not rich and poor, bond and free, but they were all made free, and partakers of the heavenly gift.

When you summarize your own experiences in three words and insert them in the margins of your scriptures, you become another witness of the truth of those scriptures. Imagine the power that would come into your daily scripture reading by having hundreds of your own experiences come to mind as you read principles. Those words testify that you know the principles are true and help to make each day meaningful.

Notes

1. Bruce R. McConkie, "The How and Why of Faith-Promoting Stories," *New Era*, July 1978, 5.

2. Henry D. Moyle, in Conference Report, Apr. 1959, 96–98.

3. Joel Hawes, *Treasury of Spiritual Wisdom* (San Diego, CA: Blue Dove Foundation 1996), 105.

4. Michael Cioppa, *Success Is Not a Miracle: The Science of Achievement* (Lincoln: iUniverse, 2003), 8.

5. Gene R. Cook, *13 Lines of Defense: A Guide for Clean Living in an Unclean World* (Salt Lake City: Deseret Book). Talk on CD.

6. Ezra Taft Benson, "To the 'Youth of a Noble Birthright,'" *Ensign*, May 1986, 43.

7. N. Eldon Tanner, in Conference Report, Oct. 1974, 122.

CHAPTER 7
Search, Ponder, and Pray

B. H. Roberts: "It is so generally the case that the revelations the Prophet received came in response to inquiries either by himself or by those who sought to learn their duty or to know some truth, that such inquiries may be considered as a condition precedent to his receiving revelations."[1]

We live in a world so full of noise that it is hard to find quiet time to ponder what course we should take in life. In most cases, the noise appears to be self-inflicted. Many get up in the morning and turn on various devices that blast spirit-deafening noise to distract them from the new day. Multiple voices in society vie for our attention and lure us into focusing on things that are anything but "virtuous, lovely, or of good report or praiseworthy" (Article of Faith 1:13). During a typical day, we may find it difficult to avoid thinking about crime, war, political corruption, protest, natural disasters, school shootings, plane crashes, high profile scandals, and so on. Mixed in with these are messages from alluring advertisements and entertainment that tell us how happy we could be if we behaved as others do. We are inundated by advice from "experts," ever ready to tell us how to view every social, legal, religious, sports, or political issue. Social media sites entice us to spend an inordinate amount of time on trivia—watching prank videos gone viral or trying to get to the next level of the latest game. Spending too much time listening to the noise of the world leads to "ever learning, and never able to come to the knowledge of the truth" (2 Timothy 3:7). We will seldom learn anything of lasting value by spending our time listening to the noise of worldly voices.

Instead, we have available at our fingertips inspired counsel given by ancient and modern prophets. It is at our fingertips but is not usable without effort; the Lord expects us to find out how to apply it to the circumstances of our own lives. How do we do that? We ask the Lord questions and then, in a quiet attitude of meditation, we ponder the answers as the Spirit whispers.

Rarely does God give revelation—even to His prophets—without a question being asked first. The Church came back to the earth because a young boy asked which church to join. The answers Joseph Smith received have blessed the lives of millions on both sides of the veil.

Joseph was confused and frustrated as he listened to the various arguments of religious groups where he lived. Identify the five questions he was pondering as recorded in Joseph Smith History 1 (emphasis added):

10 In the midst of this war of words and tumult of opinions, I often said to myself: *What is to be done? Who of all these parties are right; or, are they all wrong together? If any one of them be right, which is it, and how shall I know it?*

Notice how he paid a price to get his answers; he said those questions were "often" on his mind. Pondering great questions often is the way to learn great lessons. Now look for the next crucial part of the formula for receiving answers:

11 While I was laboring under the extreme difficulties caused by the contests of these parties of religionists, *I was one day reading* the Epistle of James, first chapter and fifth verse, which reads: If any of you lack wisdom, let him ask of God, that giveth to all men liberally, and upbraideth not; and it shall be given him.

When Joseph read this scripture, he still had questions, but already the Lord was beginning to offer answers. Joseph described it this way:

12 Never did any passage of scripture *come with more power to the heart* of man than this did at this time to mine. It seemed to *enter*

with great force into every feeling of my heart. I reflected on it again and again, knowing that if any person needed wisdom from God, I did . . .

Even before his vision, Joseph was already being touched in a powerful way by the Holy Ghost, who urged Joseph to pay attention to this particular scripture. To this point, Joseph has "labored under extreme difficulties" and pondered and studied to receive answers to his questions. Similarly, you must pay a price to have those experiences that will reassure you God is listening.

Even though James 1:5 came with "great force" into Joseph's heart, that scripture does not actually answer any of his five questions. But it does supply another critical piece of the formula for getting the answers. He had been working hard, asking himself questions but the answers were still not coming. The scripture in James taught him that he wasn't asking the right person. He needed to quit asking himself and ask God.

13 At length I came to the conclusion that I must either remain in darkness and confusion, or else I must do as James directs, that is, *ask of God.* I at length came to the determination to "ask of God," concluding that if He gave wisdom to them that lacked wisdom, and would give liberally, and not upbraid, I might venture.

14 So, in accordance with this, my determination to ask of God, I retired to the woods to make the attempt. It was on the morning of a beautiful, clear day, early in the spring of eighteen hundred and twenty. It was the first time in my life that I had made such an attempt, for amidst all my anxieties I had never as yet made the attempt to pray vocally.

Joseph acted on what he felt inspired to do, and that is another part of the formula. Needing privacy, he picked a quiet secluded place—a grove near his home, which became sacred that day. Alone in the grove, he asked the Lord to answer his questions. Even then, the Lord allowed this young man to have a terrifying experience with the adversary before finally giving him the answers. That day, in a grove in New York, "the stone was cut out of the mountain without hands" and began to roll forth (Daniel 2:45). Now millions of prayers with similar inquiries are answered because a young boy went into a quiet grove and asked the Lord with faith for answers and received them.

We learn from this that the Lord does not give out answers easily. He expects us to pay a price and follow the procedures He has in place. Not all of our questions are as critical and life changing as Joseph Smith's were that day. But the steps he took to get his answers are universal. Remember, he started off by pondering important questions.

In 1902, French sculptor Auguste Rodin finished the first large-scale bronze casting of a statue called "The Thinker." It was unveiled to the public in 1904 and became the property of the city of Paris. It is now housed in the Rodin Museum. The statue depicts a man sitting with his elbow resting on his knee and his chin atop his hand. His expression indicates that he is engrossed in deep meditation and seems oblivious to his surroundings. We would all be better off if we spent more time in such a state of contemplation. Many arise and proceed to the action portion of the day without taking time to ask and ponder in a spirit of prayer about how the day should unfold.

When America declared its independence in 1776, an estimated 2.5 million people were living in the colonies. Among them were some of mankind's greatest political thinkers and visionaries. How is it that Thomas Jefferson, John Adams, Benjamin Franklin, Alexander Hamilton, John Hancock, George Washington, Patrick Henry, and James Madison (to name just a few) were able to have such a profound influence on a newborn republic? They asked important questions and pondered, discussed, debated, and sought divine guidance to the answers. Hamilton explained it, "Men give me some credit for genius. But all the genius I have lies in this. When I have a subject in mind I study it profoundly. Day and night it is before me. I explore it in all its bearings. My mind becomes pervaded with it. The result is what some people call the fruits of genius, whereas it is in reality the fruits of study and labor."[2]

Today, approximately 320 million people live in America, 128 times the population of our nation when it was founded. It should follow that we now have at least 128 times the great political thinkers and visionaries pondering ways to improve and preserve the nation. In fact, we should have far more than that with access to all the knowledge gained from the past and the free flow of information in the present. There are plenty of brilliant minds that have discovered ways to make extraordinary improvements. But can you name the great political thinkers of our day, the ones focusing on the social, cultural, and financial issues that threaten our republic?

What is the difference between 1776 and today? Perhaps if we would all turn off the noise for a while and assume the position of "The Thinker," we could get answers to the hard questions we face as individuals, families, and society. President Harold B. Lee shared this quote from President David O. McKay, who said, "We don't take sufficient time to meditate. I get up early in the morning . . . , five o'clock, when my mind and spirit are clear and rested. Then I meditate. You can come closer to the Lord than you imagine when you learn to meditate. Let your spirits be taught by the Spirit."[3]

An important thing to pray about is how to raise a righteous family in a wicked world. You have the benefit of correct gospel principles but you still need to figure out, with the Lord's help, how to handle specific situations. In some instances, you will have a long period of time to ponder and pray while at other times the path your feet take must be decided upon quickly. That means you must spend time in your sacred grove getting direction to take *before* the time when you have only seconds to decide.

When President Henry B. Eyring was called to the First Presidency, an article about his life appeared in the *Ensign*, written by Elder Robert D. Hales. In that article is an account of how President Eyring's wife, Kathleen, handled a situation with two of their sons. She obviously had pondered and prayed about the skills of a good mother, but she learned as we all do that there are not always textbook answers to the questions of parenting.

> Henry J., the oldest son [of Elder and Sister Eyring], recalls an experience that made a significant difference in the spirit of the Eyring home.
>
> "My brother and I were in front of the TV one Saturday night around midnight," says Henry J. "A tawdry comedy show that we shouldn't have been watching was on. The basement room was dark except for the light from the television. Without warning, Mother walked in. She was wearing a white, flowing nightgown and carrying a pair of shears. Making no sound, she reached behind the set, grabbed the cord, and gathered it into a loop. She then inserted the shears and cut the cord with a single stroke. Sparks flew and the set went dead, but not before Mother had turned and glided out of the room."

Unnerved, Henry J. headed to bed. His innovative brother, however, cut a cord from a broken vacuum and connected it to the television. Soon the boys had plopped back down in front of the television, hardly missing any of their show.

"Mother, however, got the last laugh," Henry J. says. "When we came home from school the next Monday, we found the television set in the middle of the floor with a huge crack through the thick glass screen. We immediately suspected Mother. When confronted, she responded with a perfectly straight face: 'I was dusting under the TV, and it slipped.' "

President Eyring honored his wife's wishes, the children honored their mother's desires, and that was the end of television in the Eyring home. "For the most part, Mother leads through quiet example," Henry J. observes. "However, she is also inspired and fearless. Mother's assertiveness has been a great blessing to her children and grandchildren. Both in pivotal moments and in daily routines, she has forever changed the course of our lives."[4]

Sister Eyring had firmly fixed in her mind the direction she and her husband wanted to take their family. I'm fairly certain that she did not learn in some college parenting class to cut the TV cord with shears or "dust" under the TV. After realizing there was a problem, Sister Eyring pondered her options and perhaps even asked the Lord what to do to solve the problem. That decisive action, in the words of her son, "forever changed the course of our lives."

One of the most profound scriptural messages is found in the book of Proverbs: "Ponder the path of thy feet . . ." (Proverbs 4:26). Ponder means to appraise, think about, reflect upon, consider, or deliberate. Someday, you will find yourself in situations like Sister Eyring did, where there is no clear answer found in a Google search. What a great comfort it is to know that you can have answers to your questions if you pose a specific question, ponder the answer over the course of time, and then turn to the Lord for help and guidance. Then don't forget to record the answers you receive to make your day even more meaningful.

I remember a time in life when I had a question that was on my mind frequently. I wanted to know how I could do a better job of keeping the spirit in my life and staying motivated. I thought about it often, but no specific answers came. Finally, after pondering the question for weeks, I asked the Lord for help in the quiet of the early morning. I didn't receive a direct answer to my question then, but I felt prompted to go through my old journals. I found the following three entries:

February 10, 1982

It's paying off. The getting up early—spending time with the children and the physical exercise is changing my whole attitude. I have seen things in a whole new light and can feel myself becoming a new person. Isn't it amazing how if we halfway try, the Lord blesses us in amazing ways? It seems like every day I'm learning things that I have never even dreamed of before. I have finally begun to carry a memo book around with me to write down the ideas I have during the day. I have wanted to do this for quite a while but never have got around to it. I have found so many opportunities to help friends in the Church since I started my "eliminating procrastination" program. I thank my Heavenly Father for the great things that He has helped me with. I have set goals for myself that I didn't believe I would ever even be interested in trying to accomplish.

May 29, 1983

Sometimes to get motivated I must feel total disgust with myself. This is the feeling I have with myself today. I feel very unworthy of all the great blessings I enjoy. I can't believe how quickly I can go from a spiritual high to the opposite. What's so depressing about it is that I know what the problem is. Without fail, a lack of self-discipline leads to discouragement. It starts off innocently: a little too much to eat, sleep in a little later than is needful, put off physical fitness. And all of a sudden, I have no patience with the kids and feel terrible with myself. Then I start seeing faults in others and I'm right back to the natural man. It's always a challenge to stay motivated enough to read my scriptures in a meaningful way, to get up early, and to stay in good physical condition. I've found that it's a lot easier to keep up the commitment when you have it going than to try to start it up again once you have lost it. However, I'm recommitting today to try and do better.

June 1, 1983

Well, my last entry a few days ago found me low and discouraged. Now I feel excited and happy. What is the difference? Again, I have proven to myself what it takes to help me get motivated to action and feeling spiritual.
- Get up early in the morning
- Start the day off studying the gospel and planning the day
- Maintain a physical fitness program
- Control my appetite
- Work hard during the day
- Pray for help

I guess I should have these points engraved on my forehead because of the number of times I have discovered them and then lost them again. Hopefully, making this entry will remind me of what I need to do to maintain a spiritual high. Having self-discipline increases one's happiness and helps bring the Spirit into our lives. When I fail to subdue myself, I am unhappy and lose the Spirit. Every time I try to do the things the Lord commanded me to do, I am immediately blessed.

The answers to my question—answers I already had—were found in these journal entries where the Spirit guided me to look. When I do those six things, inspiration is more likely to come and I more easily recognize the grand lessons around me that make meaningful days. While not always totally successful, I have tried hard to follow those six practices. It helps to recognize why I have gotten off-track and how to get back on. God was patient in pointing me to the answers he had already given me years before. And because I had recorded those answers, the lesson was more quickly available to me.

The Lord was similarly merciful to Oliver Cowdery when he asked a question he already had an answer to: "Verily, verily, I say unto you, if you desire a further witness, cast your mind upon the night that you cried unto me in your heart, that you might know concerning the truth of these things. Did I not speak peace your mind concerning the matter? What greater witness can you have than from God?" (D&C 6:22–23).

In my many years as an institute director for the Church Education System, I have had plenty of opportunities to ponder the challenges of college students. One thing that has been troublesome to me is the staggering student debt that so many take on. Many students do not work while pursuing their degrees and depend on loans to live. Unfortunately, some of them are pursing degrees in fields that, in many cases, do not lead to a job at all, let alone a career that will help them pay those debts. President Gordon B. Hinckley gave this counsel, "I urge you . . . to look to the condition of your finances. I urge you to be modest in your expenditures; discipline yourselves in your purchases to avoid debt to the extent possible. Pay off debt as quickly as you can, and free yourselves from bondage."[5] I have pondered many times over this question: Heavenly Father, how can I teach these students to avoid debt as much as possible and to be wise with their finances?

One day at lunchtime, I was in my office and John, a married student, came in to visit and eat his lunch. Soon two other students joined us. As we ate, John told us how good his takeout lunch was and urged us to try the restaurant near campus. One of the other students asked him how often he ate out for lunch. He replied, "Every day." He then mentioned that his wife, who was also a student, did the same thing. I was a little surprised, as I knew that they were taking out student loans. The other student asked him how much the lunch cost. John replied that his sandwich and chips cost $6.95 and the specialty drink was $2.95. When everyone left, I wrote down his totals and added tax, which brought the total to $10.74. I then multiplied that number by 30, which brought his total to $322.20 a month if he actually did that every day. I was a mid-career professional, brown bagging it with my lunch from home. John and his wife, living on student loans, were spending around $644.40 a month just for lunch.

I also knew that several other students had similar eating habits. I wanted to somehow convince them to follow the teachings of our prophets concerning money. I knew I couldn't just quote general authorities about the dangers of debt; the students had heard it all before. And many of them would counter, "It's okay to go into debt for an education."

Elder Tad R. Callister said that asking good questions would help: "The power of a good question is of inestimable worth. In many ways, it is like a mental alarm clock that awakens us out of our mental doldrums. It is a catalyst that jump-starts our mental engines. It causes the cerebral wheels to move, and thrusts upon us a certain uneasiness, an anxiety that triggers a fixation on the subject at hand until relief comes only in the form of an answer that is both satisfying to the mind and acceptable to the heart."[6]

During the same time I was pondering the question of John and his lunches, I was also teaching a class called "The Gospel and Productive Life," and I had a lesson coming up on money management. So I formed a question and took it to the Lord: How can I teach the college students in my class to be wise with their money and avoid unnecessary debt?

One day before teaching that class, I was mulling over my question while driving to buy groceries at a local wholesale club. My errand was to buy enough food for a month, along with some extra for food storage. An idea came into my mind that I should compare the amount I spent that day to the $322.20 that John would spend for lunch in a given month. Here is what my receipt reflected that day:

8#	Beef Brisket $12.00	4	Loaves Bread $5.28
5#	Hamburger Lean $12.90	12	Fresh Bagels $3.86
4#	Chicken Tenders $12.82	10#	Pancake Mix $5.66
3#	Bacon $8.26	1	Large Syrup $2.93
3.5#	Beef Franks $6.33	25#	Pinto Beans $13.22
5#	Pork Tenderloin $8.40	5#	Green Beans $5.22
10	Pack Tuna $6.46	5#	Frozen Corn $4.08
6#	Bananas $1.90	4#	Broccoli Florets $4.32
5#	Gala Apples $5.97	37oz	Box Cereal $4.84
10#	Carrots $4.54	48	Granola Bars $8.28
5#	Onions $3.27	87oz	Cinnabon Mix $4.97
20#	Potatoes $7.72	50#	L. Grain Rice $11.19
3	Dozen Eggs $4.84	45oz	Spaghetti Sauce (3) $6.86
72	Cheese Slices $7.38	8#	Bag of Spaghetti $5.88
3	Gallons Milk $10.35	25#	Flour $8.47

Total: $208.20

The day I taught the institute class on money management, I used a "hypothetical" situation of a student who bought a sandwich, chips, and specialty drink every day for a month and I told the class how much it would cost. I then put up a PowerPoint slide of my shopping list from the wholesale club. I had spent $114.00 less on food for my family for an entire month that the hypothetical student would spend for just lunch. I then asked the class how many of them could afford a personal chef to cook for them every day. No hands went up. But isn't that exactly what we do when we eat out every day?

My wife and I try to go on a weekly date, so I next showed my class a slide with exactly what we had spent on entertainment that month. I pointed out that it was far more than normal that month because we had splurged on a traveling Broadway play.

- 2 Matinee Movie Tickets: $13:00
- 2 Dinners at Maude's: $19.00 (Includes Tax and Tip)

- 2 Dinners at Chili's: $18.00 (Includes Tax and Tip)
- 2 Tickets "Phantom of Opera": $64.00

Total Date Night: $114.00
Total Groceries: $208.20
Total: $322.20

It was an instructive coincidence that my total monthly date night and grocery budget added up to John's monthly lunch bill, even before counting his wife's lunches. I don't know how many of the students were affected by the lesson, but I do know the Lord taught me a meaningful lesson that day.

The following is a journal entry from Pamela, who was one of my students at BYU. She spent an hour pondering a very good question: How can I be more Christlike for the next week?

I began my day by pondering what I could do to become more Christlike. After about forty-five minutes I felt that my list was complete—too complete. One would think that I was trying to become perfected within the week. With the will to do better came a more apparent knowledge of all that I have to improve on. The following list contains the ideas of action I felt inspired to write down:
- Abstain from Diet Coke
- Abstain from crass language
- Abstain from all deceit
- Abstain from gossiping
- Abstain from R-rated movies
- Abstain from inappropriate music
- Look to serve more—especially with visiting teaching
- Pray more earnestly
- Early to bed and early to rise
- Practice patience
- Be more open with my mother
- Be more sensitive to the sacredness of the Sabbath day
- Strive to be more organized

Well, the first day was illuminating. Many times I caught myself about to make a slanderous or gossipy comment in passing and had to stop myself. But the most obvious and neat thing that happened today occurred on my way to exercise.

Every night I go to the Smith Fieldhouse on BYU campus to run. While driving to the track, I usually turn on my radio to some bebop station to get my blood pumping, to psyche myself up for a great run. Well, on this night, I turned on the radio to the song "Relax" by

Frankie Goes to Hollywood. This song has got an awesome melody. But as I listened to the words I was singing, I immediately felt that the song was not appropriate for this week especially, or any week for that matter. The words were awful.

Upon arriving at the track, I could not get the words out of my head. The longer I ran, the more prevalently they came. I was feeling sick. I prayed to Heavenly Father to help me rid this awful song from my mind. Within two minutes, for the life of me, I could not remember the name of the song I was struggling to forget or any of the words to it. Wow!

Nathan, another one of my students, similarly vowed to spend a week constantly asking what Jesus would do in a given situation. Here is one simple experience he had that week:

Today while I was running, I passed a guy in a desolate part of town where the railroad tracks cross under the freeway. I could tell that he was a little physically and mentally impaired. He was walking with his shirt off and I was a little uncomfortable passing him because of the location. I passed him and hurried at a quicker pace to put distance between us, when suddenly the question popped into my mind: "What would Jesus do?" I turned around and even though I was a little worried, I went back and asked him if he was all right. He looked really surprised as I asked the question and said, "Yes." Then he told me his name and I told him mine and I felt (I know this is going to sound weird) an instant friendship or love for him. I turned around and kept running and looked back occasionally to be sure that he was all right.

I learned the most important thing tonight. To do what Christ would do means to always be thinking of others, and to do for them all that you can, even giving your life for them. But many times it's the small things that are the hardest but most rewarding. If I could only experience ahead of time the feelings I would feel when I do what Christ would do, I would always do good. But I guess I wouldn't have learned what I did this week if it were that way. I know I'll never forget the question: "What would Jesus do?" And hopefully I'll always do it. It's been the best week I've had in a long time.

Nathan did not do anything dramatic. He simply turned around and introduced himself to a man he did not know. The results, however, were very dramatic as he felt a friendship with and love for a total stranger. As he becomes more Christlike, Nathan might be prompted in ways to help that stranger, but even in this first brave step he learned a lesson that needed to be written down. Elder Theodore M. Burton said: "Much of what we now regard as scripture was not anything more or less that men writing of their own spiritual experiences for the benefit of their posterity."[7]

Remember, there is rarely a revelation without a question first being asked. I challenge you to get out a pen and paper or an electronic device and write down a good question related to something that you need help with. Spend time pondering the question and seeking answers through your own mental efforts and from the Lord in prayer. When specific ideas begin to come, write them down and act on anything you are specifically told to do. After you act, record the results of what you learn.

Notes

1. Smith, *History of The Church*, 5:XXXIV.

2. Sterling W. Sill, in Conference Report, April 1957, 108.

3. Harold B. Lee, *The Teachings of Harold B. Lee* (Salt Lake City: Bookcraft, 1996), 130.

4. Robert D. Hales, "President Henry B. Eyring: Called of God," *Ensign*, July 2008, 13–14.

5. Gordon B. Hinckley, "To the Boys and Men," *Ensign*, Nov. 1998, 52–54.

6. Tad R. Callister, "Teaching the Atonement," *Religious Educator*, Vol. 3, No. 1 (2002): 56.

7. Theodore M. Burton, "The Inspiration of a Family Record," *Ensign*, Jan. 1977, 17.

CHAPTER 8

A House of Learning

Robert D. Hales: "Temples are the greatest university of learning known to man, giving us knowledge and wisdom about the creation of the world. Washings and anointings tell us who we are. Endowment instructions give guidance as to how we should conduct our lives here in mortality."[1]

My mother is a temple worker at the Houston Texas Temple. One day, she was standing by her post near the recommend desk when the front doors opened and a little boy about four years old stood there alone. His parents were enjoying the grounds outside and apparently didn't realize he had walked through the door. The boy looked at my mother and asked, "Is this Jesus' house?" My mother replied, "Yes, it is." The little boy then exclaimed, "Well, I've come to see Him!"

This child seemed to have learned at a young age that a person goes to the house of the Lord to be taught by Him. Perhaps we as adults get so focused on doing vicarious work for the dead that we sometimes forget that it is also the greatest place to learn lessons for those on this side of the veil. Many years ago, Elder Rudger Clawson gave this valuable insight: "The temple of God . . . is the connecting link that connects the heavens with the earth."[2]

One of the remarkable stories in the life of Jesus Christ occurred when He was twelve years old. Joseph and Mary had taken their family to Jerusalem to celebrate the Feast of the Passover. During the return trip, they discovered that their young son was not among their kinsfolk as they had supposed. They quickly returned to Jerusalem to find him. The record then states, "And it came to pass, that after three days they found Him in the temple, sitting in the midst of the doctors, both hearing them, and asking them questions. And all that heard Him were astonished at His understanding and answers" (Luke 2:46–47). As a boy the age of our latter-day deacons, Jesus was already teaching in the temple. Even the doctors of the day were astonished at the answers they received from Him. Today, as we seek to learn essential lessons, surely we should attend the temple and seek answers from the master teacher.

During a testimony meeting while I was serving as a bishop, one of the sisters in our ward shared an experience she had had with her daughter, Jessica. This daughter had come to me as soon as she turned twelve to obtain a limited-use temple recommend so she could serve as a proxy in baptisms for the dead. For months, her parents drove her to the temple every Saturday for that. Her mother said that as they were driving home on one weekend, Jessica turned to her and said, "Mom, when I'm in the temple I feel like I never want to do anything wrong in my life." What a great statement about the power of the house of the Lord to teach. The temple is a place where the Lord reveals Himself to mortals.

I've heard many times over the years that we go to the temple once for ourselves and for the rest of our lives for others. While that statement is true when it comes to proxy temple ordinances, it may cause a misunderstanding about what is available if we attend the temple with a desire to learn. Jessica not only felt the joy of doing work for others. She also learned that when she is in the temple, she wants to be a better person. We should always go to the temple with a desire in our hearts to bless the lives of those who have passed on, but we should also remember that we are there to be taught by the Lord:

> Behold, this is the tithing and the sacrifice which I, the Lord, require at their hands, that there may be a house built unto me for the salvation of Zion—
>
> For a place of thanksgiving for all saints, and for *a place of instruction* for all those who are called to the work of the ministry in all their several callings and offices;
>
> *That they may be perfected in the understanding* of *their ministry*, in *theory*, in *principle*, and in *doctrine*, in *all things pertaining to the kingdom* of God on the earth, the keys of which kingdom have been conferred upon you. (D&C 97:12–14; italics added)

Attending the temple will help bring a beautiful spirit into our lives and will give us a place to receive instruction. If we want to feel what Jessica felt, we should go to the temple often, seeking to be taught by the Lord. President Howard W. Hunter made this significant statement about the temple: "And we again emphasize the personal blessings of temple worship and the sanctity and safety that are provided within those hallowed walls. It is the house of the Lord, a place of revelation and of peace. As we attend the temple, we learn more richly and deeply the purpose of life and the significance of the atoning sacrifice of the Lord Jesus Christ. Let us make the temple, with temple worship and temple covenants and temple marriage, our ultimate earthly goal and the supreme mortal experience."[3]

I have also learned that it is not just the work that goes on inside temple that teaches remarkable lessons, but it also applies to anything to do with the work for the dead. On January 8, 2003, my wife, Wendy, our daughter Natalie, and her fiancé, Steven, traveled from Texas to Illinois to take our daughter Nichelle to the Joseph Smith Academy, where she'd attend a BYU semester in Nauvoo. Afterward, we continued toward Winter Quarters Visitors Center in Nebraska, where Natalie had served her mission. On the way, we stopped in Lewis, Iowa (population 433), where Wendy's 3rd great-grandparents, William and Sarah Richardson, had lived. She wanted to try and find the cemetery where they were buried to obtain dates from the tombstones so their temple work could be done. We stopped at a small post office and asked for directions to the nearest cemetery.

After arriving at the cemetery, we discovered that it was much larger than expected. It was divided into five sections. We each took one section and agreed to meet at the fifth section if we didn't find their gravesite. There were hundreds of tombstones and many were unreadable from years of deterioration or were covered with algae. I started out with great enthusiasm, wanting to be first to find the needle in the haystack but soon became discouraged when it appeared hopeless. We had no luck and all ended up in section five. I was convinced the search was futile and was ready to go. I went up to Wendy to tell her we needed to get back on the road. She was standing in front of a tombstone covered with algae. She used her foot to clean off the algae but still could not read it. Just to show my wife that we had at least tried, Steven and I used some branches to clean it off more. Soon we saw the names William Richardson (d. 3 Dec.

1885) and Sarah Griggs Richardson (d. 30 July 1887). Tears were shed and pictures were taken. Needless to say, it was also an amazing day when Wendy and I completed the ordinances for William and Sarah in the Houston Texas Temple a few months later. From this experience in the cemetery and also the day at the temple, I learned that many of those who have passed beyond the veil are anxious to have their temple work done and are allowed to help us find a way to make this work possible.

Elder Robert L. Simpson taught something important when he said, "The temple is a house of revelation—yes, continuing revelation. Whether that revelation be to a prophet or a member who seeks after truth, all who come to the temple seeking are continually taught and edified."[4] I know this is true because when I have gone to the temple seeking, I have been taught and edified on multiple occasions. One thing I was taught that has been edifying to me is that the temple can be a model for our own homes.

For many years, our family lived in a neighborhood where I drove by a model home every day. Wendy and I had been in that model home, and in other model homes, to get decorating ideas for our own home. Of course, model homes usually contain every upgrade offered by the builder and are professionally landscaped and decorated. The purpose of models is to show buyers the kind of home they can have if they are willing to pay the price. The world certainly needs such a model at this exciting yet very dangerous time in history. President Gordon B. Hinckley said, "Perhaps our greatest concern is with families. The family is falling apart all over the world. The old ties that bound together father and mother and children are breaking everywhere. We must face this in our own midst. There are too many broken homes among our own. The love that led to marriage somehow evaporates, and hatred fills its place. Hearts are broken, children weep. Can we not do better? Of course, we can. It is selfishness that brings about most of these tragedies."[5]

I have learned over time, that the temple can be a model home to help us build strong families. We are taught in the Bible Dictionary, "A temple is literally a house of the Lord, a holy sanctuary in which sacred ceremonies and ordinances of the gospel are performed by and for the living and also in behalf of the dead. A place where the Lord may come, it is the most holy of any place of worship on the earth. Only the home can compare with the temple in sacredness"

(Bible Dictionary, "Temple," 780–81). Surely while we attend the temple we should look for ways the temple can help us with our own homes.

Wendy and I have been fortunate enough to attend sessions in every temple in the United States. While each temple has unique features, they also have many things that are the same. Every temple has a recommend desk, endowment rooms, sealing rooms, a celestial room, and a baptismal font sitting atop twelve sculpted oxen. And the instruction received in every temple is the same. Our homes, like temples, also have unique features, but the Lord has revealed a pattern upon which both the temples and our own homes should be based. He said, "Organize yourselves; prepare every needful thing; and establish a house, even a house of prayer, a house of fasting, a house of faith, a house of learning, a house of glory, a house of order, a house of God" (D&C 88:119).

I would like to share a few of the lessons that I have learned while looking at the temple as a divine model home to strengthen families. When entering the grounds of the temple, there is a feeling of peace and serenity. It is as if you have left the world and are entering a sacred place. The temple grounds are immaculately kept and the exterior of the buildings are also beautiful and well maintained. If we are looking to the temple as our divine model home, we learn that our yards should be cared for and the exteriors of our homes should be well maintained also. Do the grounds of your home have the same feeling as those of a temple? Do family members and visitors feel as if they are leaving the world and coming to a safe place when they come to our homes? President Spencer W. Kimball counseled, "Keep in good repair and beautify your homes, your yards, farms, and businesses. Repair the fences. Clean up and paint where needed. Keep your lawns and your gardens well-groomed. Whatever your circumstance, let your premises reflect orderliness, beauty, and happiness."[6]

When a temple is dedicated, it is consecrated to the Lord, or offered up to Him for His use by proper priesthood authority. There is always a tremendous spiritual outpouring at these special events. A feeling of reverence also comes into a temple after it has been dedicated. Our homes can and should also be dedicated as sacred edifices. The Church Handbook of Instruction 2, which is available at lds.org, states this in section 20.11:

Church members may dedicate their homes as sacred edifices where the Holy Spirit can reside and where family members can worship, find safety from the world, grow spiritually, and prepare for eternal family relationships. Homes need not be free of debt to be dedicated. Unlike Church buildings, homes are not consecrated to the Lord.

When you walk into any temple, immediately you see a recommend desk. Those working at the desk are instructed to greet you with a smile and to make you feel welcome in the house of the Lord. What a difference it would make if every person who entered our homes felt loved and welcomed.

William Taylor gave this touching description of how Joseph and Hyrum Smith greeted each other: "Never in all my life have I seen anything more beautiful than the striking example of brotherly love and devotion felt for each other by Joseph and Hyrum. I witnessed this many times. No matter how often or when or where they met, it was always with the same expression of supreme joy."[7]

After greeting patrons, temple workers at the recommend desk verify the worthiness of those entering by checking to make sure every person has been interviewed and found worthy to enter. While we don't have home recommends, fathers—as the priesthood leader of their homes—should conduct regular interviews with family members. What a great protection it would be to their children if fathers regularly asked children questions that would prepare them to obtain a recommend in the future. Children would be reminded of the standards honored in that home, just as showing a recommend at the door of the temple reminds you of the standards expected of those who enter.

While President Ezra Taft Benson did not use the term *recommend desk*, he did say that parents should also be at the *crossroads* when it comes to their families. He said, "Take time to always be at the crossroads when your children are either coming or going—when they leave and return from school—when they leave and return from dates—when they bring friends home."[8]

There is a critical reason to be at the crossroads when your children are coming and going. By doing so, you can check the countenances of family members. After living with someone over time, you can usually learn to read his or her countenance. You know if they are happy or sad or upset. That is important because it is very unusual for a child to go from saint to sinner overnight. Rather, it occurs gradually. If you can catch sin in the early stages, it is more likely that you can help prevent it from going further. Those parents who are always at the crossroads for their children are in a good position to read their countenances and see the signs of trouble early on. I've learned that a parental goodnight kiss and a hug not only show love but are strong deterrents in preventing sin.

I have also noticed that the interior of a temple is extremely clean and orderly. There is a place for everything and everything is in its place. President Spencer W. Kimball gave this counsel: "We ask you to clean up your homes . . . [and] we urge each of you to dress and keep in a beautiful state the property that is in your hands."[9] It is easier to feel the Spirit when your surroundings are clean and orderly.

The pictures that adorn the walls of temples also help bring the Spirit. In the temple, you will find pictures of Christ, scripture scenes, and scenes from nature. These are reminders of whose house it is and what it represents. What pictures decorate the walls of your home? Your bedroom? President Ezra Taft Benson said, "Enter the homes of those who have been born again, and the pictures on their walls, the books on their shelves, the music in the air, their words and acts reveal them as Christians."[10]

A friend of mine, Richard, was asked to be a tour guide during the Oklahoma City Temple open house. He took a woman of another faith, who was ninety percent deaf, through the tour. She asked him to speak directly into her ear during their time together. As the tour progressed, Richard explained the purpose of each room. As they entered the celestial room, he advised her that there would be no talking there, but apparently she did not hear him. As the group walked in, this good woman walked directly under the chandelier, made four turns, and said loudly with each turn, "Ooh!" Finally, she pronounced for all to hear, "I've died and gone to heaven!" The temple does give us a taste of heaven in a physical environment, which allows it to be a house of learning.

Every temple in the Church is presided over by a president, with counselors and a matron and her assistants. In other words, there is someone is in charge of the day-to-day temple operation to make sure that the temple runs smoothly while following established guidelines. These men and women are chosen by the Lord and are experienced, trained, and inspired to guide the affairs of that temple.

Temple workers are integral to the Lord's house, but they do not share the authority of the temple presidency. I have learned from the temple model that parents need to be in charge of making sure their homes run smoothly. They are also called by the Lord and entrusted with His children. Even though children play an integral role in each family, they don't have the authority or experience to make the important decisions for the family.

It is also important to realize that temple presidents do not have the authority to change the rules of the Lord's house. Let's imagine for a moment that you and your spouse are called to be the president and matron of a temple. You ponder how to increase attendance and several ideas quickly come to mind. You could eliminate the recommend desk so no one is impeded from entering. You could open the temple seven days a week; Sunday is the Lord's day, so why not open His house on His day? And what better family home evening could you possibly have than to attend the temple on a Monday night? People are busy, so if you pared the endowment session to forty-five minutes, patrons could double their productivity.

This of course would never happen in our temples. The Lord set the guidelines for temples and reveals them through His prophet. The temple president is responsible for seeing that the temple runs smoothly while following all of the rules established by the Lord. Why is it that some parents feel they have the right to change the rules the Lord has revealed to His prophets for the home? When the prophets teach rules such as no dating before age sixteen, no steady dating during teen years, no inappropriate movies, no immodest clothing, no profanity, and so on, do LDS parents then have the right to alter those inspired guidelines?

President Gordon B. Hinckley taught, "It is interesting to reflect on the fact that although many on the other side may not receive the ordinances done for them here, those who perform these ordinances will be blessed in the very process of doing so."[11] For me, looking at the temple as a model for my own home has been a great blessing. So many things can be learned if we will take the time to look closely for ideas just as you would at a model home.

Every time I go to the temple with a question, I seem to learn something. It is amazing how many grand lessons come when questions are asked within the temple walls and how meaningful each day becomes. I would like to share one experience from my journal that happened in the San Antonio Temple by asking the question: What lesson can I learn from this?

January 30, 2014

Today was a very special day working at the temple. I learned many valuable lessons. We had a beautiful young couple come in to be sealed for time and eternity. Ivan was a lifelong member and Carol was a convert to the Church. They came from a small branch in South Texas. His mother came and sat in the waiting room until time for the sealing, but no one else traveled to the temple for this special occasion. They had no escorts, no witnesses, and no friends to witness the sacred marriage ceremony. This was a stark contrast to the large groups that recently attended temple marriages. And yet this couple radiated the same extreme happiness as those with large numbers of friends and relatives in attendance. I think everyone who met them could not help but be struck by the intense love and respect they had for each other.

Being the shift coordinator, I assigned myself and another temple worker named Ron to serve as their witnesses. After some papers were signed, the young couple walked in and sat down next to Ivan's mother. There were two temple workers in the room and an older man who had been in the sealing room when they came in. He had asked if he could stay when he saw what was happening.

Brother O'Banion, the temple sealer on our shift, gave them some wonderful instruction before having them kneel across from each other at the altar. He told them that he did not want them to look at him during the ceremony but to look at each other. Tears filled their eyes. Their looks reflected love, honor, respect, and virtue. Everyone in the room got emotional watching them as they knelt across the altar. I saw the older man wiping away tears even though he had never met the couple before they walked into the room. It was a powerful spiritual experience for me and, I'm sure, for everyone in the room.

As I watched this young couple, I reflected back to other temple marriages I have witnessed over many years. I think all of the couples looked at each other about the same way Ivan and Carol did today. That seems to be what happens when you are worthy to marry the Lord's way. So what grand lesson did I learn today as they were kneeling there? I learned that Ivan and Carol and every other couple who have ever knelt across the altars of the temple had better be very careful if they want to keep that same intense love and respect for each other in the future. Why? Because several of the temple marriages I witnessed in the past have ended in divorce and bitterness. Selfishness in many cases destroyed those marriages and led to lives being affected in negative ways. Unfortunately, the pain came at the hands of those who looked at each other the same way Carol and Ivan have today. I realized again that the marriage relationship is different than the love that a mother feels for her newborn. That powerful and enduring love seems to be a natural thing between a mother and her own flesh and blood. It is extremely difficult to destroy a love between a mother and child. That does not appear to be the case between husband and wife. To keep the love burning strong, couples must be fiercely loyal to each other while putting the happiness of their spouse first.

Every time I go to the temple with the right attitude and seek answers, I come away with something meaningful. We have discussed previously the benefits of asking specific questions and pondering to find answers. There is no better place to do that than in the house of the Lord. President Hinckley also made these wonderful promises to those who faithfully attend the temple: "If there were more temple work done in the Church, there would be less of selfishness, less of contention, less of demeaning others. The whole Church would increasingly be lifted to greater heights of spirituality, love for one another, and obedience to the commandments of God."[12]

Notes

1. Robert D. Hales, BYU Devotional Address, Nov. 15, 2005.

2. Rudger Clawson, in Conference Report, Apr. 1933, 77–78.

3. Howard W. Hunter, in Conference Report, Oct. 1994, 118.

4. Robert L. Simpson, "The House of the Lord," *Ensign*, Oct. 1980, 10.

5. Gordon B. Hinckley, in Conference Report, Oct. 1997, 94.

6. Spencer W. Kimball, "Family Preparedness," *Ensign*, May 1976.

7. William Taylor, *Young Woman's Journal*, XVII, Dec. 1906, 547–48.

8. Ezra Taft Benson, *Teachings of Ezra Taft Benson* (Salt Lake City: Bookcraft, 1988), 515.

9. Spencer W. Kimball, "God Will Not Be Mocked," *Ensign*, Nov. 1974, 4.

10. Ezra Taft Benson, in Conference Report, Oct. 1985, 6.

11. Gordon B. Hinckley, Temple Presidents Seminar, Aug. 15, 1989.

12. Gordon B. Hinckley, *Teachings of Gordon B. Hinckley* (Salt Lake City: Deseret Book, 1997), 622.

CHAPTER 9

A Protection from Serious Mistakes

Millennial Star, 1840: "*Do you keep a Journal?* If so, well—and you will have your reward; and if not, we would again enjoin it upon you, and upon all who have not before heard the admonition, to commence forthwith to keep a Journal, or write a history; and see to it, that what you write is strictly true and unexaggerated; so that in the end, all may know of all things concerning this last work, and all knowledge may flow together from the four quarters of the earth, when the Lord shall make his appearing, and we all may be ready to give a full account of our mission, our ministry and stewardship, and receive the welcome tidings, 'Thou hast been faithful over a few things, I will make thee ruler over many things; enter thou into the joy of thy Lord.' "[1]

We live in a world where we are bombarded with messages that portray sin as appealing and fun, with no apparent negative consequences. We face tremendous pressure from the crowd to join in things that are inappropriate. Yet the consequences can be dire. Elder Jack H. Goaslind said, "Sin is sin because it destroys instead of saves; it tears down instead of builds, it causes despair instead of hope."[2]

Something that helps protect us from that destruction and despair is recording our daily actions and their consequences in a "true and unexaggerated" way. One day, we will stand at the judgment bar and give a full account of our mission, ministry, and stewardship while on the earth. Imagine the joy of hearing the Lord say, "Well done, thou good and faithful servant: thou hast been faithful over a few things, I will make thee ruler over many things: enter thou into the joy of thy lord" (Matthew 25:21).

A short time after making my commitment to keep careful records of my experiences and the lessons learned from them, I was sitting in a BYU class thinking about ways to keep my family close to the gospel. Something my professor said that day hit me hard and I immediately wrote it down in a pocket notebook I had started to carry with me. He said when he and his wife were first married, they chose a family motto that would help guide their future decisions: "Be where you are supposed to be, when you are supposed to be there, doing what you are supposed to be doing." After class, I returned to our basement apartment and told Wendy that I wanted to use this same motto for our family. She agreed and over the years we have repeated that motto hundreds of times to each other, our five children, and ourselves. Because I took the time to jot down a few words, we followed up on that impression and have been blessed as a family.

I was reminded of the far-reaching effect of that motto one night in Arizona many years ago:

I am in Arizona doing a series of talks. Yesterday, I spoke to the seminary students at Dobson High School in Chandler at the request of a friend. My topic was on being a good example. It seemed to go well. Last night, I spoke at a CES-sponsored "Know Your Religion" series on parenting at a stake center in Mesa. After the talk I had nothing to do, so I decided to go see a movie that several LDS friends had highly recommended. I had read several reviews and knew that the message was positive and uplifting. President Gordon B. Hinckley has encouraged us to go to good movies when they are in town so as to encourage those who produce them to make more.

I had checked a local paper earlier to find a location where the movie was playing and found a theater in Tempe, near where I am staying. As I walked up to the ticket booth, I noticed the large poster showing the PG-rated movie I had come to see. I also saw a poster advertising a popular R-rated movie that was highly acclaimed and recommended by several movie critics. The poster made the movie look extremely appealing. I thought about how tempting this situation could be for some people. Here I was 1,200 miles from my home in Texas and I didn't know one person in the entire area. The adversary is quick to whisper in these situations that the movie is not really bad since it is historical and no one would ever know which movie you went to see anyway.

Make Every Day Meaningful

I am thankful for the family motto that a BYU professor shared one day in class. I'm also very grateful for the protection that comes knowing I am going to write about my experiences and account for my actions. Of course, there was no way I was going to go against our motto and watch an R-rated movie when President Ezra Taft Benson has specifically counseled us to avoid them. At the ticket booth, I told the teenage worker I wanted one ticket for the PG movie that I had come to see. When I told him the name of the movie, he smiled as he got my ticket and took my money. It was as if he was pleased with my choice. I couldn't help but wonder why he cared which movie I saw. As he handed me the ticket, he said, "Thanks, Brother Wright." I was a little shocked since I did not recognize him and I was so far from home. To my knowledge I didn't know one person in Tempe, Arizona. I asked him how he knew my name. His response will always stay with me. He said he was at the talk I had given to the combined seminary classes at the Dobson High seminary the day before. As I walked into the movie theater, I thanked my Heavenly Father for helping me not be tempted to go against my beliefs. I wonder what the young man would have thought if I had made a different choice.

Looking back on that experience makes me grateful again for our family motto *and* for a written account. This practice of recording the experiences of life has helped me many times as I remind myself that I would never want to do anything that I would be embarrassed or ashamed of recording.

Andrew Jenson, who served for many years as an assistant Church Historian, made this thought-provoking statement about the important role personal records can make in protecting us from making mistakes: "The keeping of a journal has a tendency to keep both mind and body in the straight and narrow path. If we keep a journal we naturally desire to write something that will read well. We want to make a good record of ourselves. But in order to do so we must live a good and useful life, and thus by our actions produce materials for a clean and interesting record. We might falsify our records, but, as record makers we would constantly think of the recording angel who is making a true history of all our actions; and if we felt convinced that our record did not correspond with his in the main, we should not feel comfortable."[3]

Imagine writing any of these in your journal for posterity to read:

- Today I drank a margarita at the company party because my boss offered it to me.

- Last night I watched a pornographic movie on television after everyone went to bed.
- I turned in my taxes and hope the IRS never finds out that I understated my income.

It helps me to picture my grandchildren reading one of my journals in the future and saying to their siblings, "Hey everyone, listen to this . . ." I want to record things that will help teach them and build their testimonies. To do that, I need to live not only my public life but also my private life in strict harmony with the gospel. Josephine Washburn said, "My diary is not at all private, but lies on the table, in the room, where all who wish may look at, and refer to that which may be of interest to them."[4]

One semester, while I was teaching in the religion department at BYU, our class discussed the difficulty of avoiding sin and temptation and overcoming weaknesses. I assigned my students to live seven days with one question constantly in mind. And they were to write a daily one-page account of their experience. The question was: What would Jesus do in this situation? Not wanting to be a hypocrite, I joined them for the assignment. We began the experiment by spending an hour thinking about our weaknesses and the things that most often tempted us to sin. We were to write down the areas we needed to work on. Most students found the week very rewarding, and yet difficult at the same time. Here is a journal entry from Pamela:

I am on day four of trying to live like the Savior for one week. One thing I decided to do this week was avoid seeing any R-rated movies. Tonight I was supposed to go on a double date to see *The Butcher's Wife* since it was not rated R. (I had stated on the phone that I could not see an R-rated movie.) About an hour before I was to go on the date, I felt great trepidation, anxiousness, and even sadness welling up inside me. I wasn't completely sure why this was, but I decided to ask my brother for a blessing. In the blessing, Heavenly Father emphasized many times that I must be an example to those around me. He said that people look to me more than I realize and that I must be careful in how I choose to act and speak. He kept warning me to be strong, to not buckle under peer pressure. I couldn't understand why this was being said to me so prevalently and at this particular time. I felt like I was past buckling under any peer pressure. At about that time, I got this strong feeling that something would happen on the double date and we would only be left with the option of seeing an R-rated movie.

Make Every Day Meaningful

As it turns out, we got to the movies too late to see *The Butcher's Wife* and were left with few options. Everybody else wanted to see *For the Boys*, and I love Bette Midler, but the movie was rated R. Immediately, I could feel Heavenly Father prompting me to take a stand and say that I would not be able to see the movie. At the same time, I could feel Satan's constant prodding to give in. Well, to my shame I gave in. I went in and watched the movie with my date and the other couple. There was no nudity, but the language was horrendous and the vulgar insinuations were nonstop. I sat in the theater completely sick to my stomach. I felt the terrible gnawing feeling of having let my Heavenly Father down. I just wanted to go home. I could not wait for the date to be over. The movie finally ended and I went home as quickly as I could without being overtly rude. I learned two things that night. I first learned that R-rated movies are not a Christlike activity. Second, I learned that no one at any age is above peer pressure.

I'm sure Pamela wasn't proud to report the events of that day, trying as she was to live like the Savior, but I'm glad she was honest in sharing her experience and what she learned from it. When you record mistakes made, even if you are circumspect in including the details of serious sin or if you destroy the record later, the act of recording will allow you to closely examine the chain of events that led up to the action and can help prevent it from happening again. Consider what happened to Pamela as she:

- Wrote a specific goal to not see an R-rated movie that week
- Felt trepidation and anxiousness before her movie date
- Asked her brother for a blessing and was admonished to be an example to others
- Was warned in the blessing to be strong and stand up to peer pressure
- Felt like she was "past buckling under any peer pressure"
- Had a strong feeling she would face the temptation that night
- Felt prompted by Heavenly Father to take a stand
- Felt Satan's prodding for her to give in
- Gave in to the pressure she felt and ended up seeing an R-rated movie
- Felt ashamed, sick to her stomach, and felt a gnawing feeling during the entire movie
- Felt as if she had let down her Heavenly Father

111

What was Pamela's biggest mistake? Was it watching an R-rated movie or was it ignoring the counsel received in the priesthood blessing and multiple promptings from the Spirit? The Book of Mormon points out another potential mistake on the path to sin. When Corianton was immoral with the harlot Isabel while serving as a missionary, his father Alma said where he had gone wrong: "Now this is what I have against thee; thou didst go on unto boasting in thy strength and thy wisdom" (Alma 39:2). Pamela, perhaps like Corianton, felt she was "past buckling under any peer pressure." Any time you believe you are past temptation, you have invited Satan to put a target on your soul.

Pamela did not commit as horrendous a sin as Corianton did, but she put herself in a compromising situation. She was fortunate in that her class assignment reminded her that she would be making a written record of her choice that night. That played a big part in her reaction to the movie. And it had the potential to help her avoid future bad choices. Knowing that you are a recorder of your daily actions can help you avoid wrong choices.

When President Thomas S. Monson was called into the First Presidency in 1985, an article appeared in the *Ensign* giving a brief history of his life, written by Elder Jeffrey R. Holland, who was then serving as President of Brigham Young University. The article begins with this experience:

> Twenty-three-year-old Tom Monson, relatively new bishop of the Sixth-Seventh Ward in the Temple View Stake, was uncharacteristically restless as the stake priesthood leadership meeting progressed. He had the distinct impression that he should leave the meeting immediately and drive to the Veterans' Hospital high up on the Avenues of Salt Lake City. Before leaving home that night he had received a telephone call informing him that an older member of his ward was ill and had been admitted to the hospital for care. Could the bishop, the caller wondered, find a moment to go by the hospital sometime and give a blessing? The busy young leader explained that he was just on his way to a stake meeting but that he certainly would be pleased to go by the hospital as soon as the meeting was concluded.
>
> Now the prompting was stronger than ever: "Leave the meeting and proceed to the hospital at once." But the stake president himself was speaking at the pulpit! It would be most discourteous to stand in the middle of the presiding officer's message, make one's way over an entire row of brethren, and then exit the building altogether.

Painfully he waited out the final moments of the stake president's message, then bolted for the door even before the benediction had been pronounced.

Running the full length of the corridor on the fourth floor of the hospital, the young bishop saw a flurry of activity outside the designated room. A nurse stopped him and said, "Are you Bishop Monson?"

"Yes," was the anxious reply.

"I'm sorry," she said. "The patient was calling your name just before he passed away."

Fighting back the tears, Thomas S. Monson turned and walked back into the night. He vowed then and there that he would never again fail to act upon a prompting from the Lord. He would acknowledge the impressions of the Spirit when they came, and he would follow wherever they led him, ever to be "on the Lord's errand."[5]

Because President Monson recorded this in his journal and was willing to share it with Elder Holland thirty-five years later, others can learn this powerful lesson about following spiritual promptings. Like my student Pamela, President Monson has felt the sick, gnawing regret that comes from a poor choice. A future prophet procrastinated in following the prompting of the Spirit as we all have done, but was wise enough to allow that mistake to change his life. By recording your mistakes, you can better analyze what happened and how to avoid making the same mistakes in the future. If you fail to record the lessons you learn in life, you are more likely to keep repeating them over and over. King Benjamin told his people that had it not been for the teachings preserved in their written records, they would have become like the Lamanites, "who know nothing concerning these things" (Mosiah 1:5).

Our natural inclination may be to fill our journals with our shortcomings and struggles. It is as important to also record the consequences of right choices. Reading back on the positive feelings that come when we do what the Lord would have us do can be a powerful motivating force for good. For example, Colby, an LDS policeman, recorded this experience,

After graduating from Utah State, my wife and I moved to Texas so I could attend the Austin Police Academy. One day, an instructor informed us that he wanted each cadet to stand alone in front of the class and sing a song. The thought of singing a capella in front of other cadets of course made me feel uncomfortable. The purpose, he said, was to help bring us out of our comfort zone and help us learn to use forceful voices. As police officers, we are often required to use forceful, authoritative voices in tense situations.

As cadets one by one sang the Marine's Hymn, the Air Force and Army songs, and alma mater fight songs forcefully, I wondered what I should sing, having never served in the military like many others had. Surprisingly, the song that came to mind that day was "Called to Serve." I wondered if I would have the nerve to passionately sing that song in front of guys who didn't exactly share my same background or religious beliefs.

Eventually, about half of the cadets had volunteered to sing and half of us had not. When there was a lull in the volunteers, our trainer informed us that if we didn't sing today that the next day we would have to sing for twice as long and so on for as many days we put it off. At that point I raised my hand to get it over with.

As I stood before my fellow cadets, I told them that I had never been in the military but I would sing a song that I often sang as an LDS missionary. Unfortunately, I didn't have an entire zone of missionaries singing along with me and was probably a little off-key, but I did my best to sing it forcefully.

I would love to say that the song had a powerful impact on the others in the room that day, but I don't know that. I do know, however, that singing "Called to Serve" definitely forced me out of my comfort zone and helped alleviate my fear of sharing my beliefs. Since that day, I have become close friends with many of the cadets and had a number of conversations about the Church and my mission. After standing up and singing an off-key solo to the group, I have found that answering questions about the Word of Wisdom and polygamy is not nearly as nerve-racking as it used to be.

I hope that Colby's posterity will read this record one day. He learned that we are often prompted by the Spirit to take a stand for what we believe in. Perhaps his written account of what happened then will be the very thing his descendants need to help them have the courage to get out their comfort zone and stand up to pressure. His experience also will teach them that they can do it without causing offense or losing friends. In fact, it appears that Colby may have attracted a few friends because of his heartfelt song.

Keeping a written record not only helps you avoid inappropriate situations, but it also encourages you to do worthwhile things. The bottom line is that if you would be embarrassed to write your actions for others to read, then don't do it! Charlotte Perkins Gilman put it this way: "It was my definite aim that there should be nothing in my diary which might not be read by anyone."[6]

Notes

1. The *Millennial Star*, Vol. 1, Oct. 1840, 160–61.

2. Jack H. Goaslind, "Happiness," *Ensign*, May 1986.

3. Andrew Jenson, *Collected Discourses 1886–1898*, ed. Brian Stuy, vol. 5. (Burbank, CA, and Woodland Hills, UT: B.H.S. Publishing, Jan. 20, 1895).

4. Josephine Washburn, "Keeping a Line Diary," *Harper's Young People*, Apr. 22, 1890, 11:431.

5. Jeffery R. Holland, "President Thomas S. Monson: Man of Action, Man of Faith, Always 'On the Lord's Errand,'" *Ensign*, Feb. 1986, 11.

6. Charlotte Perkins Gilman, The *New England Magazine*, Vol. 11, Issue 5, Jan. 1892.

CHAPTER 10

Overcoming Weaknesses
That Limit You

Bryant S. Hinckley: "When a man makes war on his own weaknesses he engages in the holiest war that mortals ever wage. The reward that comes from victory in this struggle is the most enduring, most satisfying, and the most exquisite that man ever experiences. In no other conflict is there so much at stake. In no other struggle are the values so precious and the results so compensating and so comforting."[1]

One of the great duties of this life is to identify one's weaknesses and turn them into strengths. I have found over time that this is not an easy task, even though the promised blessings of doing so are worth any effort required. Benjamin Franklin, one of the founding fathers of the United States, is considered by many to be a polymath, meaning he had gifts and talents in multiple areas of life. Franklin was a prominent politician, inventor, author, political philosopher, diplomat, satirist, scientist, printer, postmaster, musician, activist, and statesman. He left behind an impressive list of accomplishments. In 1726, at age twenty, he came up with a plan to overcome his personal weaknesses and improve his character. It came after he attended a Presbyterian worship service and heard the minister use Philippians 4:8: "Finally, brethren, whatsoever things are true, whatsoever things are honest, whatsoever things are just, whatsoever things are pure, whatsoever things are lovely, whatsoever things are of good report; if there be any virtue, and if there be any praise, think on these things."

Franklin was greatly disappointed with the sermon that followed because he thought the minister did not emphasize the points from the verse that were most important. Franklin reportedly never went back to that church again. However, the experience did seem to motivate him to come up with his own plan of improvement. He wrote, "It was about this time I conceiv'd the bold and arduous project of arriving at moral perfection. I wish'd to live without committing any fault at any time; I would conquer all that either natural inclination, custom, or company might lead me into. As I knew, or thought I knew, what was right and wrong, I did not see why I might not always do the one and avoid the other."[2]

Franklin's plan for overcoming weaknesses and reaching a state of moral perfection was to focus on thirteen virtues that he considered most desirable. He felt acquiring one virtue would assist him in developing the next, so he put them in a specific order. He included the name of the virtues and their precepts in his autobiography:

1. Temperance: Eat not to dullness; drink not to elevation.
2. Silence: Speak not but what may benefit others or yourself; avoid trifling conversation.
3. Order: Let all your things have their places; let each part of your business have its time.
4. Resolution: Resolve to perform what you ought; perform without fail what you resolve.
5. Frugality: Make no expense but to do good to others or yourself, i.e., waste nothing.
6. Industry: Lose no time; be always employ'd in something useful; cut off all unnecessary actions.
7. Sincerity: Use no hurtful deceit; think innocently and justly; and, if you speak, speak accordingly.
8. Justice: Wrong none by doing injuries, or omitting the benefits that are your duty.
9. Moderation: Avoid extremes; forbear resenting injuries so much as you think they deserve.
10. Cleanliness: Tolerate no uncleanliness in body, clothes, or habitation.
11. Tranquility: Be not disturbed at trifles, or at accidents common or unavoidable.
12. Chastity: Rarely use venery but for health or offspring, never to dullness, weakness, or the injury of your own or another's peace or reputation.
13. Humility: Imitate Jesus and Socrates. [3]

Franklin explained the method he developed to achieve his goal: "I made a little book, in which I allotted a page for each of the virtues. . . . I determined to give a week's strict attention to each of the virtues successively. Thus, in the first week, my great guard was to avoid every the least offence against *Temperance*, leaving the other virtues to their ordinary chance, only marking every evening the faults of the day."[4] According to this plan, Franklin would have achieved "moral perfection" in thirteen weeks.

Soon after beginning his project, Franklin realized that overcoming weaknesses and acquiring new virtues was far more difficult than he had anticipated. He said, "I soon found I had undertaken a task of more difficulty than I had imagined. While my care was employ'd in guarding against one fault, I was often surprised by another; habit took the advantage of inattention; inclination was sometimes too strong for reason."[5]

Franklin freely admitted later in his life that he did not always live up to the virtues he listed. In fact, he fell short many times. However, he always believed that his attempt at perfection made him a better person and the process contributed to his success in life.

There are a couple of factors that he failed to take into account when he first developed his plan. First—as he quickly discovered—was the difficulty of overcoming deep-seated weaknesses. Another was that he misjudged the time it would take to turn weaknesses into virtues. We all wish that we could master a new virtue every week and boast at the end of a year that we had turned fifty-two weaknesses into strengths. While it may be highly desirable, it is not feasible. In most cases, the battle to eliminate weaknesses is often an extended struggle.

Several years ago, I pulled out some of my old journals and reread past entries. My goal was to see if I had made any progress over the years. I quickly skimmed entries recorded over several years. Two related entries caught my attention and taught me that overcoming weaknesses is a difficult proposition.

January 21, 1982
Last Monday, Wendy and I finished listening to a cassette tape called Eliminating Self-Defeating Behaviors by BYU professor Jonathan Chamberlain. I also purchased his book on the subject. The idea is

to choose a behavior to work on that you feel is holding you back in your progression. Dr. Chamberlain and other researchers have spent years developing techniques to help people overcome these behaviors. It is a powerful program. I chose procrastination as the self-defeating behavior that I would most like to eliminate in my life.

As part of the program, I had to write when and how often I did this behavior. It was hard to admit how often I procrastinated and the clever rationalizations I came up with to justify my behavior. What I discovered is that I do it all the time, in all kinds of circumstances. I also identified the things I thought of before and after doing this defeating behavior. But the real eye-opener was counting the cost of hanging onto the behavior. It was a real revelation to me to see how much a self-defeating behavior can stop the progress of your life. Since finishing the tape and book, I have become very aware of the problem and have a desire to eliminate it from my life. I feel good that I have accomplished a great deal since beginning the program this week.

Like Ben Franklin, I decided that I was going to spend a week working to overcome my procrastination and record my progress in my journal. In the days that followed, I recorded with satisfaction that I was actually eliminating procrastination from my life. Looking at the entries for the weeks that followed, I saw that procrastination was mentioned less and less until it eventually disappeared from my journal. I then noticed that my journal writing became less frequent. Finally, I came to an entry dated more than fifteen years after my first written resolve to eliminate procrastination. It jumped off the page at me that day and taught me many valuable lessons:

October 27, 1997
Lately I have been reading a book called *Eliminating Self-Defeating Behaviors* by Jonathan Chamberlain. It has been sitting in my bookcase untouched for years. I remember working on some self-defeating behaviors long ago, but I can't remember what they were. Something told me that I should go through the process again and try to eliminate a behavior that seems to be holding me back. The biggest problem I have right now in my life is that I am a huge procrastinator. I put off everything you can think of. I was very aware today of my problem and how much it is holding me back. I don't procrastinate nearly as much at work as I do at home. I should be getting much more done at home and during my free time than what I do. I think I use the excuse that I try to work hard during the day so I need to relax when I get home.

> I am going to face this problem again, but it will not be easy and I know it. I have hung onto it for so long that it is going to be very hard to overcome. I did get a lot done today, however, and I hope tomorrow to face my problem even more. If I could just stay aware, I believe I could lessen the behavior in my life.

I was still struggling with the same weakness fifteen years later and had even forgotten my earlier attempt to eradicate it! One of the most important things I learned was recorded in the last sentence of the second entry: "If I could just stay aware . . ." Reading those two journal entries side by side and seeing the reason for my failure—the inability to remain aware of my goal—motivated me to start a new journal. This one is simply my "weakness journal," in which I list my shortcomings along with the strengths I want to cultivate. It reminds me of my goals and allows me to track my progress.

I also learned from this experience that a virtue for a week did not work any better for me than it had for Franklin. I thought back to something I heard at a training meeting in St. Paul, Minnesota, while I was working for the 3M Company. The presenter said something tongue and cheek that got a laugh out of those in attendance. I realize now that his statement was not far from the truth. He said, "A person twenty-one years old or older will continue to do in the future as they have done in the past unless they have a spiritual experience or brain surgery!"

I also learned from reviewing my journal that if I was going to overcome the weaknesses that were holding me back, I would have to involve the Lord. I couldn't do it on my own. President Dieter F. Uchtdorf counseled, "God wants to help us to eventually turn all of our weaknesses into strengths, but He knows that this is a long-term goal. He wants us to become perfect, and if we stay on the path of discipleship, one day we will. It's OK that you're not quite there yet. Keep working on it, but stop punishing yourself."[6]

The Lord made this remarkable promise to those who turn to him for help: "And if men come unto me I will show unto them their weakness. I give unto men weakness that they may be humble; and my grace is sufficient for all men that humble themselves before me; for if they humble themselves before me, and have faith in me, then will I make weak things become strong unto them" (Ether 12:27). You have read the promise, but do you trust it?

The following are two journal entries from Nathan, a returned missionary and BYU student at the time he wrote them. His assignment was to spend an hour in prayer and meditation trying to involve the Lord in identifying the things he needed to change in his life and the virtues he needed to acquire. As you read the two entries on successive days, look closely to see what lessons you can learn from Nathan.

Monday

Sitting in the comfort zone of my own room, I never thought an hour of quiet time to be potentially destructive of my "comfort zone" in my personal, spiritual life. I began the hour with a prayer, asking for guidance in how I could be more Christlike and sat with a pen in hand awaiting some minor suggestion on how to fine-tune my life. Little did I know! But, I'm spiritually ill. I found that the things I ended up writing down were not mere modifications needed to improve upon my supposedly righteous life, but were major renovations and overhauls that I had been overlooking or perhaps subconsciously avoiding.

I found that many of my weaknesses are found in the areas of simple interpersonal human relationships. To be Christlike, I must be charitable. As I examined my treatment of others and compared it to the Christlike ideal, I found a number of discrepancies between my supposed ideal of charity-motivated behavior and my more insensitive nature. I am often void of compassion as my friends related their tales of daily hardships. But, worse yet, is a sense of ingratitude towards my friends, family, and ultimately to God. It was a humbling experience, and one much needed. If I could add one thing to my list as of now, I would add the sin of pride that had quelled me into thinking that all was well in my relationship with God.

Tuesday

The day started out in direct contrast to what I would recommit myself to this very afternoon. Early in the groggy hours of the morning, my roommate Shaun came into my room and announced that it wasn't that early at all. We had slept in. Steve, my immediate roommate, had turned off the alarm clock when it had gone off much earlier. But upon Shaun's wake-up visit, his alarm clock was flashing. I, of course, was blamed for unplugging it. Nothing could have been more irking. I responded in childlike denial and resorted to a pretty hearty shot to Shaun's leg and even a little threatening and shouting for him to get out of my room. Not ten seconds later, the phone rang for Steve. It was his fiancée, and she was soon informed of my supposed guilt in the matter. I was furious! I hadn't even been awake for a full minute and I was already steamed. Needless to say, I failed in all senses of the word. As I stomped off to the shower, I couldn't help but be ashamed of my temper. I was really out of control.

I suppose the whole morning drama was the reason that the first way I found that I could be more Christlike, when I sat down to ponder over it after work, was to be more considerate of my roommates' feelings. I feel like my success today was in apologizing to Shaun and Steve.

Reviewing his thoughts during his hour of prayer and meditation, Nathan identified charity as the virtue he most desired and his weakness as ingratitude. In his second entry, he concluded that he needed to add denial, revenge, threats, yelling, anger, and being out of control to his list of weaknesses. No wonder Elder Jacob de Jager gave this great counsel: "There is a great need to examine yourself in these matters and ask yourself the old question, 'Am I part of the problem, or do I contribute to solving the problem?'"[7]

Nathan found it would take the Lord's help and more than a week to achieve his goal of being full of charity. On a positive note, he did apologize to Shaun and Steve, motivated in part because he knew he would have to make a written account of the progress he had made that day.

Laura, like Nathan, had the assignment to consider her weaknesses and strengths. She realized during her hour of prayer and meditation that she did not love others enough and was not a good listener. Her goal for the week was to become more like Jesus Christ by treating others the way He would treat them. Even though Laura didn't always live up to her stated goals, she did have a memorable experience to relate.

Monday
I have decided to focus this week on what I know about Christ. I know he was kind to people and I know He had a sense of fairness. My goal then, based on what I know of Christ, is to love people and to listen attentively.

Wednesday
Today while Chad and I were walking to a friend's house, an old man stopped us on the street and began talking. He looked a little like a basset hound, with saggy blue eyes and wrinkled jowls. He had wire-white disheveled hair and his belly hung over his pants and stretched his sweater tight. He said, "If you younger generations can't do something, there's not going to be anything left." He went on

to explain how President Bush did not really have the flu in Tokyo when he puked. He was just nervous, the old man said, because his finances are shaky. He said the President has Swiss bank accounts and is ripping America off. We were restless and shifted from foot to foot. The man talked about politics and then switched to sewer pipe systems and offered intimate details about his own system. It was forty minutes before we were on our way again, and Chad sighed and said, "I think we just witnessed a prophet." I laughed because I knew what he meant.

When eccentric wisdom stops you in a ratty sweater and wants to chat, it's hard to come up with an excuse not to stay. I find myself thinking that it's likely Jesus would hang out in Laundromats, arcades, and carnivals just to look out for the people who walk around with no one to listen to them. There are so many people who are lonely. Even the Beatles talked about it: "All the lonely people, where do they all come from?"

Laura and Nathan learned valuable lessons from their week of recording their attempts to become more like the Savior. One thing learned was the value of giving a daily account of their successes and failures. In doing so, they were following the counsel from President Spencer W. Kimball, who said, "Get a notebook, a journal that will last through all time . . . Begin today and write in it your goings and comings, your deepest thoughts, your achievements and your failures."[8]

Record Meaningful Daily Events

Many think that the only reason to keep a personal journal is for future generations. In reality, journals can be a tremendous benefit in the here and now. On this topic, my friend Brad Wilcox made this observation: "We tell ourselves, 'Journals are for posterity.' Well, maybe my grandson will break both legs and be desperate enough for something to do that he'll pull out my dust-covered journal. But the remote possibility of such an event in the future has never been motivation enough for me to keep a journal. In my life, I had to discover that writing in my journal is valuable for me—whether my grandchildren ever read it or not."[9]

Another practice that can be a tremendous help in overcoming weaknesses is to regularly examine yourself and pinpoint why you struggle in certain areas. Some weaknesses could even be inherent because of the natural tendencies you were born with. President

Gordon B. Hinckley referred to a flaw that plagues almost everyone. He taught, "We are all inherently lazy. We would rather play than work."[10] Other shortcomings can be traced to the indoctrination received in your homes when you were growing up. In the Book of Mormon, Zeniff explained with perfect clarity why generations of Lamanites hated the Nephites: "And thus they have taught their children that they should hate them, and that they should murder them, and that they should rob and plunder them, and do all they could to destroy them; therefore they have an eternal hatred towards the children of Nephi" (Mosiah 10:17). Laman was jealous of Nephi and felt that he had been wronged and robbed of his right to govern. He let that thought canker his soul, which over time turned to hate. Instead of changing his own heart, Laman taught his children to hate. They in turn taught their children to do the same. Eventually, the reason was lost but the hatred remained.

Your weaknesses will always have negative consequences. How many hundreds of thousands of Nephites were killed over the years because Laman taught his posterity to hate them? Even Laman in his anger could not have foreseen that his hate would lead to the destruction of untold thousands of his own posterity. Closely examine the things you have been trained to believe to make sure they are in harmony with gospel teachings. If the teachings and traditions passed to you go against revealed truths of the gospel, it is imperative that you recognize and stop them from being passed on to the next generation.

While my procrastination may not have the same societal consequences as Laman's, it could certainly destroy me personally. This statement made by Joseph Fielding Smith sums up what can happen: "Procrastination, as it may be applied to gospel principles, is the thief of eternal life . . ."[11] While not every personal weakness may cost you eternal life, there is always a price to pay for holding onto your weaknesses. Here is an experience recorded by my daughter Naomi that shows both the price she paid for one of her weaknesses and the joy that came to her when she finally recognized it and took action to overcome it.

> I was sitting in a college class and we were discussing the therapeutic benefits of confessing the things that we had done wrong in our life. The teacher taught us that if we had wronged someone and not apologized, a

tremendous burden would be lifted if we would go to him or her and get the matter straight. As he taught us this principle, I immediately had an experience pop into my mind that I had never admitted to anyone. At first I tried to laugh it off because it had happened so many years before and was only with my sister Natalie. I had rationalized it away so much over the years that I made it not a big deal in my mind, or so I thought. The next two days were pure torture as I replayed the scenario in my mind over and over.

When I was eight years old, my family didn't have a lot of money and it was well known in our family that we did not waste food. One day, I got a huge spoonful of peanut butter. I took one little bite of it and then threw the rest in the trash with the spoon. I didn't think anything about it until I heard my mom asking my two brothers if they were the ones that wasted the peanut butter. I heard them both say no. Then it was my turn. "No, Mom, I didn't waste the peanut butter." Off she went to ask my little sister Natalie. Of course she said no as well. Did I mention that Mom and Dad were very big on telling the truth? Soon Dad was involved and lined up all four of us in the kitchen. He went down the row asking each of us who threw the peanut butter in the trash. Now I felt like I couldn't tell the truth. I had already lied and gotten out of it up to this point, so I thought I might as well keep going.

It slowly became very apparent that Mom and Dad weren't going to let this one drop. Now it wasn't that one of us had wasted the food, it was that someone was lying. Finally, Dad had had enough. He told us that if the culprit didn't make himself known immediately that all of us were in big trouble. He was going to count to five and then everyone was going to be in trouble. As he started the count, my five-year-old sister Natalie stepped up and said, "It was me, Dad." I had never felt such relief in my life. I remember hearing her get in a lot of trouble as I went skipping away to go and play. I know that this seems so ridiculous because it had happened twelve years before. But I simply could not get the guilty feeling that I had to go away. No matter how many times I tried to get it to go away, I knew that the only way to feel better was to call Natalie and apologize. I will never forget her laughter as she listened to me sob and tell my heartfelt apology over the peanut butter incident. And I will also never forget the immediate relief and calmness I felt after making that confession, just like my teacher had said. I found that it is much easier to confess our faults rather than carry the burden.

Naomi learned there are serious consequences when we give in to our weaknesses and fail to repent. She carried a burden of guilt for twelve years, even though she tried to do everything in her power to rationalize her behavior and suppress it. By finally correcting her mistake and recording her experience, she can relive the tremendous relief she felt as she overcame a weakness and gained the strength to face other things she may have been suppressing. Alma described the feeling this way, "And oh, what joy, and what marvelous light I did behold; yea, my soul was filled with joy as exceeding as was my pain!" (Alma 36:20).

Like Ben Franklin, you need to list the virtues you wish to acquire in this life. The 13th Article of Faith would be a good place for you to begin your quest for perfection. Using this statement or one like it as a standard will help you determine how closely your life fits with the gospel plan.

Perhaps you have discovered as I have that developing self-discipline takes focused effort on our part. President Thomas S. Monson said, "The battle for self-discipline may leave you a bit bruised and battered but always a better person. Self-discipline is a rigorous process at best; too many of us want it to be effortless and painless. Should temporary setbacks afflict us, a very significant part of our struggle for self-discipline is the determination and the courage to try again. . . . Eternal life in the kingdom of our Father is your goal, and self-discipline will surely be required if you are to achieve it."[12] Without self-discipline, we will never be able to overcome our weaknesses. And, to make every day a meaningful experience, we must use self-discipline to become better people.

Challenge:
- Purchase a journal and label it "Weakness/Strength Journal"
- Spend time in meditation identifying your major weaknesses
- Spend time in meditation identifying strengths and virtues you desire
- Spend time in meditation trying to determine why you have these weaknesses
- Pick one weakness that seems to be holding you back the most
- Count the cost you pay for that weakness
- Pray for help and develop a written step-by-step plan to overcome this weakness
- Keep a daily record of the lessons you learn as you try to become more Christlike

Notes

1. Bryant S. Hinckley, *That Ye Might Have Joy* (Salt Lake City: Bookcraft, 1965), 83

2. Benjamin Franklin, *The Autobiography of Benjamin Franklin*, 38.

3. Ibid.

4. Ibid.

5. Ibid.

6. Dieter F. Uchtdorf, "Forget Me Not," *Ensign*, Nov. 2011.

7. Jacob de Jager, "Overcoming Discouragement," *New Era*, Mar. 1984.

8. Spencer W. Kimball, "President Kimball Speaks Out on Personal Journals," *New Era*, Dec. 1980, 26.

9. Brad Wilcox, "Why Write It?" *Ensign*, Sept. 1989.

10. Gordon B. Hinckley, "Articles of Belief," Bonneville International Corporation Management Seminar, Feb. 10, 1991.

11. Joseph Fielding Smith, in Conference Report, Apr. 1969, 121.

12. Thomas S. Monson, "Pathways to Perfection," *Ensign*, May 2002, 100–101.

CHAPTER 11

Learn to Be Grateful Every Day

Wilford Woodruff: "Should we not have respect enough to God to make a record of those blessings which He pours out upon us and our official acts which we do in His name upon the face of the earth? I think we should."[1]

Several years ago, Wendy and I were sitting at a red light with one car in front of us. An older woman stood on the sidewalk to our left with a sign that read, "Homeless, Need Help, God Bless." She looked healthy enough and the local job market was booming at the time, so I was inclined to ignore her. Then I noticed the driver of the car ahead of us. He rolled down his window and threw three dollars on the ground and quickly rolled his window up. The woman picked up the money and thanked the man through his closed window. Then she walked back to the sidewalk, looked heavenward, and mouthed the words, "Thank you." I immediately scrambled to find some money before the light changed but only came up with a dollar bill. When she took my meager donation, she said, "God bless you people." I watched as she again turned her eyes heavenward and said, "Thank you."

As soon as I could, I pulled out my pocket notebook and recorded the powerful lesson I had learned. Here was a lady who was down on her luck and she was grateful for a dollar. I was up on my luck, but often forgetting to be grateful for all my blessings. I realized that I had never once thanked Heavenly Father for a dollar in my entire life. Why is it that when we are blessed with so much we forget to thank God for what we have?

Mormon, who had reviewed more than a thousand years of his people's history, was in a unique position to identify the faults of the natural man. He included in the record this sage observation: "Yea, and we may see at the very time when He doth prosper His people, yea, in the increase of their fields, their flocks and their herds, and in gold, and in silver, and in all manner of precious things of every kind and art; sparing their lives, and delivering them out of the hands of their enemies; softening the hearts of their enemies that they should not declare wars against them; yea, and in fine, doing all things for the welfare and happiness of His people; yea, then is the time that they do harden their hearts, and do forget the Lord their God, and do trample under their feet the Holy One—yea, and this because of their ease, and their exceedingly great prosperity" (Helaman 12:2).

People who are blessed with success often are not grateful for what they have and even show contempt for God in the midst of their ease and good fortune. Elder W. Eugene Hansen taught, "It has been said that the sin of ingratitude is more serious than the sin of revenge. With revenge, we return evil for evil, but with ingratitude, we return evil for good."[2]

Sadly, it is not only those who are blessed with abundance who are ungrateful. The ten lepers, whose story is recorded in Luke 17, doubtless lived in dire circumstances, yet they also were ungrateful for an astonishing act of healing by the Savior. Ingratitude is a sin that affects people of all classes. Of the ten lepers, only one came back and fell at the feet of the Savior and expressed thanks. How is it possible that nine outcasts from society with the most dreaded disease of their day were not grateful? While pondering that question, it occurred to me that perhaps all ten were extremely grateful, but only one of them bothered to say so. President Spencer W. Kimball once said, "Too often we take blessings for granted, like the sun, the air, health, and opportunity. Or we accept favors, honors, and privileges day after day as did the lepers their newfound health, without a word of thanks. We would thank the person who gives us a seat in the bus, the person who offers a ride, the friend who picks up the check after dinner, the person who does the baby-sitting, or the boy who cuts our lawn, but do we express gratitude to Him who gives us all?"[3]

One sister taught the Gospel Doctrine class in her ward Sunday School for almost five years. During that time, only a handful of people thanked her. Fortunately, those few expressed thanks on more than one occasion. I think that most in attendance did appreciate her for teaching the class, if for no other reason than they didn't have to teach it themselves. However, like the ten lepers, they didn't express that appreciation. They took it for granted that one person would put in the hours of preparation and be there reliably every week so the rest of them could sit in the classroom and be instructed.

Based on my observations in wards I have attended, on a typical Sunday far less than ten percent of attendees express gratitude to the speakers, teachers, and musicians. Over the years, I've had the responsibility of asking hundreds of people to speak at forums held for LDS college students. During that time, I have watched on multiple occasions as not one person approached the speaker afterward, even in an audience of more than fifty people! I counted it a good day if three or four students took time to thank the presenter who was there as a favor to me. I wonder how many times over the years I have been guilty of the same thing and in the process been just like the nine lepers. Why are we reluctant to express our gratitude when so many blessings are promised for doing so? President N. Eldon Tanner made this promise: "As we express our appreciation of our many blessings, we become more conscious of what the Lord has done for us, and thereby we become more appreciative."[4]

It is not only important that we verbally express our gratitude, but also that we write down things we are grateful for and the events that teach us to be more grateful. The following is a journal entry I made after returning home from a trip.

Wendy and I just returned from a nineteen-day trip to Italy, Egypt, and Israel. We first flew to Rome, where we stood at the center of the once-mighty Roman Empire and contemplated the events that had occurred there through the centuries. We saw the Colosseum and many other wonders that I had thought I would only experience through the eyes of others in books and photographs. Michelangelo's work was a display of talent that was staggering in its depth and breadth.

We then flew to Cairo, Egypt, a city of approximately 16 million people. The pyramids were breathtaking, as were the antiquities in the Cairo Museum—the magnificent King Tutankhamen exhibit and the mummy identified as Ramses the Great, traditionally believed to have been the Pharaoh of Exodus. I visualized Ramses standing toe to toe with the indomitable Moses, who was fulfilling his mission to lead the children of Israel out of bondage.

In Jerusalem, we admired the western wall of Herod's temple. The highlight of the city was the traditional Garden Tomb, where tour guides affirmed that Jesus Christ had been resurrected and appeared to Mary. The first time we entered the tomb, we could stay only a few moments because of the long lines of people waiting for their turns. Later, we went back. The tourists were gone and we had the sacred spot to ourselves. Wendy said a prayer and neither of us want to ever forget the feelings we experienced as we felt there that day.

On our last night in Jerusalem, our group traveled by bus through winding roads. Looking out the window, I could see the old walled city of Jerusalem and the magnificent Dome of the Rock. It was completed in 691 AD, making it the oldest extant Islamic building in the world. Someone on the bus started singing a beautiful song about Jerusalem. Others who knew it soon joined in. After the song, the atmosphere on the bus was hushed as we reflected on all we had seen and the lessons we had learned.

In the quiet and almost under my breath, I started to sing another song. I didn't think it was audible but then someone in front of me joined in, and before long everyone on the bus was emotionally singing together a song written by Irving Berlin in 1938, "God Bless America." I have never appreciated America as I did that night looking out over the most storied city on Earth. We all realized that night that, at least for us, there was no place on earth that could compare to home, the United States.

I wrote the details of that experience so I would never forget the gratitude I had for America that night. Often when I feel gloomy about the direction my country is headed, I reread the details of that experience and it gives me hope. The grand lesson that I learned that night did not occur in a formal classroom setting. In fact, the vast majority of the most valuable lessons I have learned were from life experiences. If I didn't write them down, they would be lost, unless something jogged my memory.

At the root of our ingratitude is failure to take the time to consciously think about all we have been given. My daughter Natalie asked her Primary class what they were thankful for. The expected comments of family, pets, Jesus, and toys came quickly. Then one little boy taught a very important lesson: "I'm grateful for V8 Splash." I had never thought to be grateful for a favorite brand of juice before. On another occasion, at an institute forum, the speaker had us hold our arms straight out and lock our elbows. Then he challenged us to pantomime brushing our teeth or combing our hair, without bending our elbows. "How many of you have ever been grateful for your elbows?" he asked. I had to admit that elbows had never appeared on any gratitude list.

Too often we are not grateful for something until we no longer have it. For example, I never appreciate electricity until it goes out for a few hours. When it comes back on, I am very grateful for a short time and then I am right back to taking it for granted. Yet if the electricity were to go off permanently, life as I know it would cease to exist. The list of what we as people take for granted is endless.

A few years ago, I was sitting in a Chinese restaurant with friends when a piece of meat lodged in my throat. I couldn't breathe and couldn't even ask for help. Finally, after a few terrifying seconds, I was able to dislodge it. That day I walked away with a greater appreciation of what King Benjamin taught when he said, "Ye should serve Him who has created you from the beginning, and is preserving you from day to day, *by lending you breath*, that ye may live and move and do according to your own will, and even supporting you from one moment to another" (Mosiah 2:21; italics added).

That experience and scripture popped into my mind again during a high priest group meeting when the teacher shared the words by President Dieter F. Uchtdorf: "We must learn, as Moses did, that 'man is nothing' by himself but that 'with God all things are possible.' "[5] The teacher asked how we could realize that we are nothing without God. I raised my hand and said, "Hold your breath."

Learning to be grateful for V8 Splash and the air you breathe helps you recognize other things that you have been taking for granted. As part of our family's 2013 Christmas activities, I wanted to do something that would help us be more appreciative of modern conveniences. The adults played what I call the elimination game. Everyone sits in a circle with common items listed on a sheet of paper (see below). Each person in the circle takes turns eliminating one item at time until every item on the list is gone. Before choosing the item, the person pauses to think of the consequences of living without that thing. When a choice is made, there is a pause before moving on so everyone is free to point out the potential negative consequences of eliminating that item. For example, when someone in our family eliminated eighteen-wheel trucks, another pointed out that hundreds of thousands of jobs would be lost. Another said that within weeks there would be mass starvation in our nation because the food delivery system would be gone.

The Elimination Game

1. Batteries
2. Email
3. Computers
4. Television
5. Traffic Lights
6. Auto Mechanics
7. Toilet Paper
8. Policemen
9. Debit Cards
10. Credit Cards
11. Printers
12. Cars
13. Tires
14. Gasoline
15. Eighteen-Wheel Trucks
16. Facebook/Pinterest
17. Recorded Music
18. Microwave
19. Washer/Dryer
20. Target/Walmart
21. Dishwasher
22. Phones
23. Restaurants
24. Toothbrush/Paste
25. Calculators
26. Blow Dryers
27. Movies
28. Football/Basketball
29. Hot Water Heater
30. Electricity
31. Air Conditioning
32. Disposable Diapers
33. Gas/Electric Heaters
34. Google
35. Light Bulbs
36. Garbage Pickup
37. Remote Controls
38. Cable Television
39. Lawn Mowers
40. Antibiotics
41. Garbage Disposals
42. Refrigerators
43. Telephones
44. Automobiles
45. Airplanes
46. Electricity
47. Texting
48. Paved Roads
49. Satellites
50. Indoor Plumbing
51. Copy Machines
52. Eyeglasses
53. Canned Food
54. Frozen Food
55. Internet
56. Shower/Bathtub
57. Shopping Malls
58. Cameras
59. Motor Oil
60. Supermarkets

As my family played, it didn't take long for us to realize our absolute dependence on many of the things on the list. Once everything was eliminated, we circled those items on the list that did not exist prior to 1776 when our nation was formed. It was a sobering wakeup call about gratitude.

Not only is there a tendency to take things for granted, but also to covet what others have. A few years ago, seven-year-old neighbor boys David and Jared were having a conversation. Jared's father heard David say, "You sure are lucky to have a turtle." There was a long pause and then he added, "All I have is a dog, a cat, and a horse." Self-help author Melody Beattie said, "Gratitude unlocks the fullness of life. It turns what we have into enough, and more. It turns denial into acceptance, chaos to order, confusion to clarity. It can turn a meal into a feast, a house into a home, a stranger into a friend. Gratitude makes sense of our past, brings peace for today and creates a vision for tomorrow."[6]

There are multiple benefits that come to those who are grateful. Robert A. Emmons, PhD, is considered one of the world's leading experts on the subject of gratitude. As a professor of psychology at the University of California, Davis, he has conducted multiple studies on the subject. In one study, he and his colleagues divided participants into three groups and instructed them to make weekly entries in a journal for ten weeks. The groups were divided into:

- Gratitude Condition Group: They were asked to record five things they were grateful for during the previous week.
- Hassles Condition Group: They were asked to write down five hassles they experienced during the previous week.
- Control Condition Group: They were asked to write down five events that had occurred in the last week, but were not told whether to focus on either positive or negative events.

The results showed that those in the gratitude group felt better about their lives overall, were more optimistic about the future, and reported fewer health problems. They also reported being twenty-five percent happier than the other participants. Another surprising finding was that the gratitude group ended up doing nearly 1.5 hours more exercise per week than those in the hassles group or the group that was simply recording events.[7] A follow-up study suggested that a daily gratitude journal led to an even greater increase in positive outcomes than a weekly gratitude record. The bottom line is that spending even five minutes a day recording things you are grateful for can increase your well-being in multiple areas. The following benefits have been associated with those who keep a daily gratitude journal:

- More optimistic
- More positive moods
- Happier
- More alert
- Less materialistic
- More spiritual
- Less self-centered
- More self-esteem
- More determined
- More friendly
- Better marriages
- More respect for others
- More friends
- Deeper relationships
- Positive toward family
- More service-oriented
- Better sleep duration
- Better sleep quality
- Fewer doctor visits
- Longer lifespan
- Fewer physical symptoms
- Less pain
- Fewer mental disorders
- Higher energy
- More exercise
- Increased networking
- Higher goal achievement
- Improved decision-making
- Increased productivity
- More generous
- More resilience
- More outgoing
- More good feelings
- Happier memories
- Less envy
- More relaxed
- More forgiving
- Less lonely

President Lorenzo Snow said that we should "always cultivate a spirit of gratitude. It is actually the duty of every Latter-day Saint to cultivate a spirit of gratitude."[8] Much later, President Gordon B. Hinckley made the following promises to those who express gratitude: "When you walk with gratitude, you do not walk with arrogance and conceit and egotism, you walk with a spirit of thanksgiving that is becoming to you and will bless your lives."[9] The Lord has also promised, "And he who receiveth all things with thankfulness shall be made glorious" (D&C 78:19). With so many blessings promised to those who have this spirit of gratitude, what can you do to help cultivate it?

I attended a priesthood quorum class where the instructor said that he had a hard time being happy. He then looked to his left and said, "I'm not like John here, who is always happy." John's four-word response was profound and life-changing for me. He simply said, "You have two choices." In other words, you can either be happy or sad. It is the same with gratitude. You have two choices.

That same week I received a Christmas card and letter from Rhonda, a former seminary student. In the highlights of the year she included this insight from one of her sons: "Patrick has been serving in the Dominican Republic Santiago Mission since July and every week his emails begin with this phrase: 'THIS has been the happiest week of my entire life.'" Patrick had learned the same lesson that John knew and we all should learn. You have two choices: be happy or unhappy.

A familiar hymn, "Count Your Blessings," written by Oatman Johnson Jr. with music by Edwin O. Excell can help you decide which choices to make. I suggest memorizing the inspired words and reciting them on a regular basis.

Illinois State EFY

Wendy and I count among our blessings the Especially for Youth programs where we have been session directors. At the 2010 session held at Illinois State University in Normal, Illinois, one of my favorite counselors was Morgan from North Carolina. During a meeting with the counselors, I taught them to constantly look for grand lessons, for those events that had made their day meaningful, and to write them down. When I got home, I received the following excerpt from Morgan's journal, in which she recorded a gratitude experience.

> During our Normal, Illinois session of EFY, there was a boy there named Tyler. I believe Tyler was high-functioning autistic. He had a huge grin on his face always and was so sweet. At the dance our last night, he came up to talk to me and started telling me how his feet were hurting. I told him that I was sorry and, with his big grin, he responded, "It's okay, I know why. Bad shoes!" I said, "Those are the worst." I then asked him if he had enjoyed his week and he replied, "Yep, but my least favorite part is coming up though." I asked, "What part is that?" "Leaving," he said. Then after a pause he added, "One week a year I get to fit in . . ." I was quiet for a minute as I thought about what he had said and then told him he was a good kid and he went off to dance. It broke my heart to think that someone feels like they only fit in once a year, but I was also really grateful at that moment that I was part of something that gave kids like Tyler an opportunity to fit in, even if it was only for one week.

Challenge:

Express Thanks in Prayer: Your most sincere and frequent gratitude should be directed toward your Heavenly Father. President Ezra Taft Benson taught, "The Prophet Joseph said at one time that one of the greatest sins of which the Latter-day Saints would be guilty is the sin of ingratitude. I presume most of us have not thought of that as a great sin. There is a great tendency for us in our prayers and in our pleadings with the Lord to ask for additional blessings. But sometimes I feel we need to devote more of our prayers to expressions of gratitude and thanksgiving for blessings already received."[10]

Keep a Gratitude Journal: No matter how many blessings you or I have, we usually are not happy until we *recognize* what we have. Spencer W. Kimball promised, "Those who keep a book of remembrance are more likely to keep the Lord in remembrance in their daily lives. Journals are a way of counting our blessings and of leaving an inventory of these blessings for our posterity."[11] The more you write about blessings received, the more you notice what you have been given. I challenge you to get a journal and make it a lifelong ritual to write down at least one thing per day that you are grateful for and why you feel that way. Be sure to also record experiences you have that teach you gratitude.

Notes

1. Journal of Wilford Woodruff, Feb. 1862.

2. W. Eugene Hansen, "Love," *Ensign*, November 1989, 24.

3. Spencer W. Kimball, *Faith Precedes the Miracle* (Salt Lake City: Deseret Book, 1972), 201.

4. N. Elden Tanner, in Conference Report, October 1967, 54.

5. Dieter F. Uchtdorf, "Pride and the Priesthood," *Ensign*, Nov. 2010.

6. Melody Beattie, *The Language of Letting Go: A Meditation Book and Journal for Daily Reflections* (Center City, MN: Hazelden Foundation, 2003), entry for August 1st.

7. Robert A. Edmonds, et al., "Counting Blessings Versus Burdens: An Experimental Investigation of Gratitude and Subjective Well-Being in Daily Life," *Journal of Personality and Social Psychology*, Vol. 84 (2), February 2003, 377–89.

8. Lorenzo Snow, *Teachings of Lorenzo Snow* (Salt Lake City: Bookcraft, 1984), 61.

9. Gordon B. Hinckley, *Teachings of Gordon B. Hinckley* (Salt Lake City: Deseret Book, 1997), 250.

10. Ezra Taft Benson, *God, Family, Country: Our Three Great Loyalties* (Salt Lake City: Deseret Book, 1974), 199.

11. Spencer W. Kimball, *The Teachings of Spencer W. Kimball,* ed. Edward L. Kimball (Salt Lake City: Bookcraft, 1982), 349.

CHAPTER 12
Meaningful Lessons Are Not Lost

Fraser's Magazine, 1859: "There are strong arguments why every man should keep a diary. I cannot imagine how many reflective men do not. How narrow and small a thing their actual life must be! They live merely in the present. . . . If a man keeps no diary, the path crumbles away behind him as his feet leave it; and days gone by are little more than a blank, broken by a few distorted shadows. His life is all confined within the limits of today. Who does not know how imperfect a thing memory is? . . . A man might almost as well not have lived at all as entirely forget that he has lived, and entirely forget what he did on those departed days."[1]

A former mission president of the Texas San Antonio mission was the chief legal counsel for a Fortune 500 company before his mission call. In a stake conference I attended, he spoke about the importance of learning from our experiences and continually improving ourselves. To illustrate, he shared this story: He and other executives in his company met to consider candidates to fill an important leadership position. Someone suggested that a long-time employee be offered the job since he had twenty-six years of experience with the company. Another executive said, "Actually, he only has one year of experience." The other committee members were puzzled. They all knew how long this man had been with the company. The executive explained, "He has one year of experience repeated twenty-five times." With that statement, the man was passed over for a major promotion. Everyone in the room understood that he was stalled in the past, not using his experience to change and progress.

When we fail to record the experiences we have in life that teach grand lessons, we tend to forget what we have learned and are "confined within the limits of today." It is as if we invent the wheel then forget how we did it and spend the rest of life trying to reinvent it. No wonder so little progress is made on our earthly journey.

If you find yourself in that situation, don't despair. Your lessons learned and unrecorded may not be lost forever. James M. Barrie, the Scottish author who created Peter Pan, said, "God gave us memory so that we might have roses in December."[2]

He also gave us memory so we could remember past lessons and use them to make personal growth. You may be thinking, "How? I couldn't even find my keys this morning." My father, who never recorded anything he learned, would often say, "I don't know whether I found a rope or lost a horse." While it may be true that your keys and horse are lost, the experiences that left deep impressions on you are safely stored on your brain's hard drive, waiting to be recalled.

Computer search engines such as Google are among the most remarkable inventions in modern history. It is almost beyond comprehension that you can find vast amounts of information in less than a second on almost any topic imaginable. However, all of that knowledge lies dormant and does you no good until you type in specific search words and press enter. These search words need to be specific to what you are searching for. You cannot type in "killer whale" and expect to get information on the score of the BYU game.

What if you could do a Google search of your brain and bring back experiences from the past that had an impact on you at the time? Imagine the progress you could make if that were possible. The good news is you can do exactly that. Almost all of your grand lessons are safely stored away in your memory and just waiting for you to recall them. You just need the right key words and the memories of the past will come back to you. Once important stories are recalled, it is critical that you write them down so you do not lose them again. Having them in front of you allows you to ponder their meaning and to learn lessons from them to help you progress.

If I use "physical scars" as my search words and concentrate for a few moments, multiple experiences come to mind. The first one brings back an incident that happened in Provo, Utah, when I was first married, attending BYU and working part-time for a company that made recreational campers. One day at work, I was assigned to grind the ends of a pile of steel anchor bolts on a large circular metal sander. The owner of the company was a close personal friend of Thomas S. Monson, who happened to be visiting my boss that day. As I was grinding away, one of my coworkers said, "Hey, here comes Elder Monson!" I was excited to get a glimpse of an apostle in person and I quickly turned to look. As I turned, my left knee went directly into the grinder, which ripped through my jeans and made a silver dollar sized gouge on the side of my knee. The pain was intense and I was miserable for many days afterward. To this day I still have a large scar that reminds me of President Monson and my carelessness.

The keyword search of my brain for "physical scars" also brings up an experience I had while speaking to a group of twelve- and thirteen-year-old boys in Anchorage, Alaska. My topic that day was making wise decisions. I used Doctrine & Covenants 9:8 as the theme and emphasized that the boys should make a habit of studying things out in their minds and praying for direction before making decisions. To illustrate my point, I asked the boys if they had any physical scars. Almost every hand went up. My intent was to teach them that many of the scars in life, both physical and emotional, could be avoided if the boys simply studied things out first and then prayed to know if what they were about to do was right. I then asked if anyone would like to share the story of scars. I won't write their entire comments; I think you can fill in the blanks.

- Boy 1: "I was sliding down the side of a mountain on a piece of tin and hit a . . ."
- Boy 2: "My brother was jumping on the trampoline and I walked under it and stood up while he was jumping. I got knocked down and . . ."
- Boy 3: "I was born with six toes on each foot and the doctor had to cut off a toe on each foot." (This boy asked if I wanted to see the scars. I told him I would take his word for it.)
- Boy 4: "I was sitting on the kitchen counter picking my nose with a knife and I fell off the counter onto the floor and . . ."

After the first two boys had made their comments, I asked the group what they could learn from the experiences that would help them in life and I repeated the formula found in Doctrine & Covenants 9:8. I reminded them that those scars could have been avoided if they had studied things out beforehand and asked if what they were doing was the right thing. Boy 3 with twelve toes caught me off guard. I had no idea how to apply my scripture theme to his case, so I thanked him for sharing and moved on to knife boy. When he told his story, the adults in the room were laughing so hard it was difficult to continue with my talk. However, I learned valuable lessons from them so they were stored in my memory. Later, I wrote down exactly what happened so I wouldn't forget the specific details from each experience.

Try an experiment to see if your personal search engine is working as it should be. Do you have physical scars anywhere on your body? Do you have more than one? If so, conjure up the memory of the oldest one. Were you doing something you shouldn't have been when you got it? How old were you? Were you afraid when the incident happened? Did you learn any lessons that day? Have you written the experience down? I guarantee that if you have physical scars you will most likely remember how you got them. If you are one of the lucky few with no scars, then there is nothing in your hard drive to retrieve. But you may remember a time when friends or family earned their scars. Could you learn any lessons from what happened to them?

I hope this little illustration has helped you see that experiences from the past are not lost and can be brought to mind using specific search words. Below you will find approximately six hundred memory cues to help you retrieve seemingly lost memories. With some cues you may not have anything stored. With others it will be like opening the floodgates as multiple experiences flow into your mind.

Memory Cues

Father	Uncles
Mother	Aunts
Sisters	Cousins
Brothers	Nieces
Spouse	Nephews
Son	In-Laws
Daughter	Ancestors
Grandfather	Children's Friends
Grandmother	Disappointed with Child

Proud of Child	Love and Affection Shown
Friendly People	Playing Games with Family
Unfriendly People	Family Difficulties
Role Models	My Curfew
Negative People	Teasing in Our Family
Positive People	Daily Family Rituals
Humorous People	Family Projects
Prejudiced People	Family Members' Quirks
Courageous People	Things Parents Taught
Cowards	Home Environment
Helpful People	Parents' Priorities
Hurtful People	Parents Away from Home
Eccentric People	Communication Styles
Easy-Going People	Negative Family Traditions
Difficult People	Positive Family Traditions
Admirable Families	Sibling Rebellion
Dysfunctional Families	Sibling Rivalry
Things Parents Did Right	Our Yards
Mistakes Parents Made	Family Pets
Things Never Told Parents	Chores or Responsibilities
Parents' Relationship	Interviews with Parents
Parents' Communication	Family Financial Situation
Times Missed Parents	Friends of Parents
Moves Family Made	Family Heirlooms
Friends of Family	Immaturity Displayed
Affection between Parents	Things Accomplished
Role of Education	Times of Family Crisis
Times Punished	Things Failed At
Teaching Moments	Maturity Displayed
Our Family Rules	Church Buildings
Santa Claus	School Buildings
Tooth Fairy	Lost Jobs
Easter Bunny	Times Unemployed
Childhood Heroes	Living on a Tight Budget
Times Parents Angry	Children's Funny Sayings
Times Siblings Angry	Worried Sick About
How Parents Treated Me	Times Surprised or Shocked
How Parents Treated Siblings	They Took Up for Me
How Parents Treated Friends	Felt Peace and Hope

Tried and Failed At	4th of July Traditions
Summer Jobs	Easter Traditions
Could Hardly Wait For	New Year's Celebrations
Wanted Revenge	Family Mealtime
Times of Forgiveness	Other Family Traditions
Felt Dread Over	Family Council
Special Hideouts	Family Punctuality
Speaking in Public	How Parents Disciplined
Local Fun Spots	Parental Expectations
No Appreciation Shown	Mothers/Fathers Day
Duh! Moments	Humorous Family Incidents
Aha! Moments	Elementary School Teachers
Times Not Prepared	Elementary School Friends
Friends Permissive Parents	Middle School Teachers
Friends Strict Parents	High School Friends
Confidences Broken	My Principals
Things Taken for Granted	Best Teachers
Stories of Early Childhood	Worst Teachers
Family Reunions	School Bullies/Rebels
Loved One's Death	Fights Watched
Family Prayer	Pranks Played
Mischief with Siblings	Eccentric Students
Houses Lived In	Excuses Used or Heard
Neighborhoods Lived In	Memorable Students
Family Drama	Special Programs or Events
Planning for Children	Students Picked On
Least Favorite Neighbors	Extra Curricular Activities
Favorite Neighbors	Cheating in School
Mistakes Siblings Made	Drug and Alcohol Users
Visitors to Our Home	Tragedy Among Classmates
Family Rules Broken	Classmates' Unwise Decisions
Punishment for Mistakes	Births Out of Wedlock
Christmas Memories	Class Reunions
Christmas Traditions	Transportation to School
Thanksgiving Memories	Parents' School Involvement
Thanksgiving Traditions	Recess and Playground
Memorable Birthdays	School Dances
Birthday Traditions	Field Trips
Thanksgiving Traditions	Most Popular Students

Visits with School Nurse
Discipline at School
Times Picked On
Times Made Fun Of
School Lunch Scene
Worst School Memories
Best School Memories
Felt Peer Pressure
Competitions Involved In
Class Clowns
Cliques at School
School Cancellations
After School Activities
Favorite Classes
Least Favorite Classes
Most Difficult Class Ever
Filthy-Mouthed Students
Sick Days
Report Cards
Science Projects
Graduation Time
School Tests
School Grades
Inappropriate Activities
Times Played Hooky
Dealings with Principal
College Preparation
College Choice
First Year of College
College Life
College Teachers
College Roommates
Leisure Time Activities
Road Trips
Concerts Attended
Drama Productions
Camping Trips
Amusement Parks
Parties Attended or Hosted

Favorite TV Programs
Favorite Movies
Water Parks/Activities
Outdoor Adventures
Movies Viewed
Favorite Songs
Impact of Music
Favorite Teammates
Least Favorite Teammates
Sports Played
Talent Shows
Games Attended
Trick or Treat
Halloween Costumes
Competitions Involved In
Sporting Events
Family Games
Vacations
Fishing Trips
Hunting Trips
Going Out to Eat
Books and Reading
Lakes, Rivers, Beaches
Historical Sites Visited
General Conferences
Firesides
How Sabbath Observed
General Authorities
Family Home Evenings
Prophets
Priesthood Blessings
Testimony Building
Book of Mormon
Temple Attendance
Welfare Projects
Missionary Work
Patriarchal Blessing
Ward Parties
Primary Songs/Programs

Sacrament Meetings
Sunday School Classes
YM/YW Activities
Priesthood/Relief Society
Reactivation Efforts
Church Teachers
My Bishops
Ward and Stake Dances
My Stake Presidents
Mission Farewells
Mission Experiences
Mission Companions
Honors Received
Scout Camp/Girls Camp
Priesthood Blessings
Church Meetings
Church Callings
Church Program Changes
Memorable Prayers
Home/Visiting Teaching
Special Baptisms
Talks Heard
Talks Given
Results of Fasting
Seminary/Institute
Personal Revelation
Results of Obedience
Faith Tried
Faith Strengthened
Word of Wisdom
Fast Offering
Service Projects
Prayers Offered
Church Sports
Puppy Love
Crushes Over Years
First Date
Casual Dating
Going Steady

My First Kiss
Memorable Breakups
Times Heart Broken
Prom Dates
Special Dates
First Love
My Courtship
Worst Date
Engagement
The Ring
The Proposal
Preparation for Marriage
Parents' Reactions
Friends' Reactions
My Wedding
My Honeymoon
Early Days of Marriage
Fun Times with Spouse
Silly Disagreements
Our First Home
Marriage Adjustment
Worst Arguments
Birth of Children
Relations with In-Laws
Anniversaries Celebrated
My Achievements
Sad Times
Happy Times
Greatest Thrills of Life
Dreams and Nightmares
Felt Humiliated
Things Worked Hard For
Was Very Shy
Things Afraid Of
Felt Very Outgoing
Significant Firsts
Viewed Human Suffering
The Day That …
Most Prized Possessions

Had Hard Feelings Toward	Gifts Received/Given
Quit and Regretted It	Results of Procrastination
Felt Depressed	Rejected Good Advice
Kindness Shown	Received Bad News
Undependable People	Received Good News
Had Mind Changed	New Year's Resolutions
Risk Taken	Personal Changes Made
Lessons Taken	How Summers Spent
Awards Received	Felt Unwise
Times I Was Gullible	Extreme Disappointment
Felt Uncomfortable	Very Excited
Bad Manners Shown	Things Made or Built
Felt Confident	Accidents Involved In
Self Discipline Struggles	Memorials Visited
Jokes Remembered	Finished Difficult Task
Kids with Bad Reputations	Unsportsmanlike Conduct
Favorite Sayings	Good Sportsmanship
With Doctors/Dentist	Doctor/Dentist Visits
Incidents with Fires	Hospital Visits
Major Storms	Happily Married Couples
Bad Habits	Marriage Breakups
Was Mocked or Teased	Close Calls
Times Felt Insecure	Sick or Injured Friends
Made Others Cry	Times Felt Motivated
Courage Displayed	National Disasters
Judged Others Wrongly	Goals Set Not Achieved
Felt Humiliation	Goals Set and Achieved
Was Disappointed In	Pain/Injury/Sickness
Mistakes Made	Worst Food Ever
Traumatic Experiences	Best Food Ever
Times Felt Lonely	Overreacted to Situation
Times Felt Included	Served As Mentor
Felt Patriotism	Observed Physical Abuse
My Quirks	Was Jealous Of
Times Physical Lost	Things Had Stolen
Times Spiritually Lost	Lack of Social Skills
Valuable Lessons Learned	Things That Irritate
Cars Owned	Hardest Job Ever
Car Problems/Accidents	My Crossroads in Life

Defining Moment of Life

Physical Scars Received

Biggest Fear

Phobias I Have

Games Played

My Heroes

Appreciate Children

Part-Time Jobs

My Bosses

My Career

Making New Friends

Mischief with Friends

Loyal Friends

Disloyal Friends

Frightening Times

Social Life

Pet Peeves

Times Didn't Think

Financial Issues

Times I Cried

Incidents with Animals

Worst Food

Best Food

My Keepsakes

Hurt by Gossip

Was Misunderstood

Lost a Friend

Felt Total Confusion

Historical Events

Personal Appearance

Physical Fitness

Felt Anger

Felt Love and Compassion

Special Homecomings

Miserable Departures

Criticism Received/Given

Kind Acts

Things Had Stolen

Dumb Decisions Made

Good Decisions Made

Embarrassing Situations

Funny Situations

Bad Experiences

My Babysitters

Fun Times

My Pets

My Personality

Others View of Me

Hardest Things Done

My Best Job

Favorite Boss

Least Favorite Boss

Worst Job Ever

Least Favorite Coworker

Favorite Coworker

Childhood Friends

Mischief with Friends

Best Friend

Others' Generosity

Others' Selfishness

My Generosity

My Selfishness

Practical Jokes/Pranks

Got My Feelings Hurt

Times I Was Late

Things I Despise

Mistakes at Work

Famous People Met

Funerals Attended

My Clothing/Style

Encounters with Police

My Hobbies/Projects

Practical Jokes Played

Volunteer Work

Physical Fitness

Personal Appearance

Sex Education Received

Self-Esteem Issues

Make Every Day Meaningful

Diets Tried
Social Problem Observed
Health Issues
Workplace Environment
Extreme Weather
Praise Received
Sleepovers
Technology Changes
Fads of the Day
National Tragedies
World Events
Political Elections
Crime Observed
Unusual Experiences
Times Gratitude Felt
Disagreements With
Regrets I Have
Power Outages
Music Concerts
I Was Misjudged
Times I Was Angry
Bad Attitude Days
Hard Times/Adversity
Irresponsible Behavior
Taken Advantage Of
Experiences in Nature
Peer Pressure Felt
Service Rendered
Grudges Held Against
People Using Profanity
Rumors/Gossip Results
Mistakes Made with Money
Times Offended
Memorable Birthdays
Cities Lived In
Least Favorite City/State
Favorite City/State
Homes Lived In
Your Bedroom

Friends' Homes
Relatives' Homes
Hotels/Motels
Hospitals
Special Getaways
Libraries
Church Buildings
School Buildings
Restaurants
Amusement Parks
Lakes, Rivers, Beaches
Air Conditioning
Refrigerators
Computers
Musical Instruments
Radios
Songs
Dances
Phones
Televisions
Movies
Stereos
Toys
Friends' Cars
Parents' Cars
My Cars
Guns
Furniture
Championships
Airports
Airplanes
Shopping
Road Trips
Inspirational Talks
Home Repairs
Extreme Stress
Uncomfortable Situations
Cooking Success
Cooking Failure

Missed School Because	Physically Lost
Got in Trouble For	"Special" Kids Known
Parents Furious	Favorite Neighbors
Missed Curfew	Least Favorite Neighbors
Rude People	Camping Trips
Ancestors	Electricity Off
Dealings with Police	My Worst Mistake
Bosses	Best Presents Received
Accidents Witnessed	Best Presents Given

Remember that it will do little good to recall experiences related to these key words if you do not write them down. When I remember a personal experience from the past or something that I observed or heard, I take a few seconds to record it in a three-word title, using a person, place, or thing to distinguish it from all other occurrences. For example, I used "President Monson Scar" and "Alaska Boys Scars" as the titles for the previous stories mentioned. One thing to remember so you do not get overwhelmed is to focus on a few memory cues per day until you have gone through all of them. Doing so will take you on a fascinating trip down memory lane. It will also be a source of tremendous knowledge and an avenue for personal growth.

Perhaps, the greatest blessing of doing this is "its power to bring back the indescribable but keenly felt atmosphere of those departed days. The old time comes over you. It is not merely a collection, an aggregate of facts, that comes back; it is something far more excellent than *that*: it is the soul of days long ago. . . . Therefore keep your diary, my friend. . . . You will look back at it occasionally, and shed several tears of which you have not the least reason to be ashamed."[3]

From the memory cues listed above, I have at least one memory in almost every category and several in some of them. For instance, the search words "embarrassing situations" trigger multiple memories. Some of them make me laugh and some make me so uncomfortable that I still want to crawl in a corner and hide. I will share one that makes me laugh now, but was not even a little bit funny the night it happened. This experience is one in which one of my children embarrassed me. From it I learned to do a better job teaching him and being involved in his activities.

Nolan Life Scout

I recently had a very embarrassing experience involving our son Nolan. I have been serving in our bishopric, which means I am also a member of our Boy Scout Committee. One of our responsibilities is to meet with the boys who were eligible for rank advancement. After meeting certain requirements, the boys appear before the Committee and have a board of review where they are asked several questions to see if they are ready to advance to the next level. On the night our second son Nolan was to appear before the Committee, I had to go to the church building early so I reminded him to wear his Scout shirt and sash and make sure he was at there on time. Right before I left, he told me that he couldn't find his Scout shirt and said that he thought someone had stolen it. I told him I was fairly certain that no one had broken into our house to steal his Scout shirt and to go find it and to be on time. I then left to join the Committee to prepare for the scheduled interviews.

When it was Nolan's turn, he walked into the room obviously wearing his older brother's Scout shirt, which was far too big. He was also wearing his brother's sash, which included many merit badges that Nolan had not earned and most likely didn't even know what they were.

The questioning began from our chairman, who just happened to be a former marine sergeant. I knew what was about to happen was going to be brutal. The first question was, "Nolan, what are the three rivers in the Three Rivers Council [the name of our Scout council]?" The Neches, Sabine and Trinity Rivers were near our home. Nolan was finally able to name one of three. I was embarrassed because fathers were supposed to have their sons ready for the reviews.

"Recite the Scout Motto."

After a long pause Nolan said that he always got that one confused with the Scout Oath. I could feel my face turning red. I hoped he would not be asked the next obvious question, but no such luck.

"Okay, what is the Scout Oath?"

Nolan replied that he always got that one mixed up with the Scout Motto. I looked down and said a silent prayer for him. This was out of my hands.

He was asked to explain the requirements for several of the merit badges he was wearing. "I got that one a long time ago and I can't remember it" was his typical answer. I felt like crawling under the table, but Nolan himself seemed unembarrassed by his performance. In the much-welcomed end of the interview he was asked what scouting had done for him. He gave a brief summary that wasn't too bad.

Finally, the chairman asked, "Nolan, is there any reason why you should be advanced to the office of a Life Scout?"

"Yes!"

The chairman asked why and all eyes in the room went to Nolan.

"Well, I knew more than I thought I would," he said.

The room burst into laughter, but it was a long time before I found the humor in it.

A few years later Nolan earned his Eagle Scout award. How did he manage it? Nolan had one quality that helped him greatly, which was that he was always where he was supposed to be. I have learned that good things happen when you are where you are supposed to be. Most success in life is just showing up and sticking to a task.

If I were to change the search words and concentrate on "Children Made Me Proud," multiple memories flood my mind. By summarizing an experience in a three-word title, I can have it available to remind me of lessons learned to use in a talk, lesson, or even in a book I may be writing. Here is an experience that made me proud of one of my children.

Naomi Widow Yard

One holiday, I was looking forward to a restful day off after a stressful week. My wife had gotten up early to go walking with a friend. When she got home, I was still in bed. She said there were tree limbs and debris throughout the neighborhood caused by high winds during the night. The widow who lived down the street was out with her walker trying to clean her yard.

At first I thought, *Let her kids clean her yard. She has plenty who live in the area.* Then the thought of her falling over in her walker moved me. I got out of bed, but I was not happy to have my day of rest interrupted. "Everyone get up!" I ordered my five children. "We're going to help our neighbor clean her yard." As we walked down the road, only my wife looked happy.

We found our neighbor attempting to clean up the rubble, using her walker to keep her balance. As we worked in her yard, she said to my eleven-year-old daughter, Naomi, "I'm just a poor widow lady and don't have any money to give you."

"You don't need to pay us," Naomi said. "We want to do this!"

I thought, *You little hypocrite. You were griping as loudly as I was a little while ago and now you're trying to be the hero.* As we raked and picked up the trash, a warm feeling began to grow inside me. I felt a spiritual lift just picking up branches and raking leaves.

Walking home after several hours of work, Naomi said, "Dad, let's do that again! I had so much fun." What she really meant was, "Dad, I like the good feeling I get when I serve others."

For many years I have had the opportunity to teach and speak to the youth and young single adults of the Church. They constantly face negative peer pressure. Knowing this, I watch for lessons learned that I think will help me teach more persuasively on that topic. I always record the lesson learned. The following are two experiences separated by many years that taught me meaningful lessons.

Elden Peer Pressure

Several years ago, I did some research on the power of peer pressure. I noticed that most of the LDS boys living in our area were part of the popular crowd at school, who all wore the same type of clothes. Many of the athletes wore Ocean Pacific (OP) T-shirts, beltless Levi's 501 blue jeans, and unlaced Nike shoes. I decided to gauge how much pressure was put on the youth to dress a certain way. I called ten boys, ranging in age from middle school through high school and asked them if they wanted to make a little money. They all said they did, but they wanted to know what the catch was. I told them I would give them each ten dollars to wear a pair of cheap plain-pocket blue jeans bought from a discount store to school for one day. The only catch was that if anyone asked, they had to say they were wearing the jeans because they liked them. Eight of the ten would not wear the jeans even though I kept increasing the amount I would give them. Several refused fifty dollars and two even refused one hundred dollars. One said, "I won't do it for any price!"

When I asked the boys why they wouldn't take the challenge, they each said, "Because everyone will laugh at me if I do."

Finally, our stake president's son, Dan (who owed me ten dollars anyway), agreed to do it. The deal was that he could pay off his debt and, at the same time, help to prove a point about peer pressure. He would wear the plain-pocket jeans for one day, but he couldn't tell anyone (at least not until the next day) why he was doing it. That night, I bought him a pair of jeans at a local bargain store and took them to seminary the next morning. Here is the report he wrote on his day's experience:

> I was hoping the pants wouldn't fit or something else would happen so everyone would know it was just a joke. All my confidence was replaced with fear as I stepped out of the car and noticed the stares

of the cheerleaders, who were standing next to the school entrance. I thought I saw them giggling at me, but I couldn't be sure.

As I walked down the hall to my first-period class, I heard someone yell behind me, "Hey, I love those pants!" When I walked into choir, about ten people burst into laughter. "Why did you wear those?" they asked, pointing at my pants. I answered, "Because I like them." The rest of the day went on in much the same way, with everyone laughing at me. This has been a real eye-opener for me concerning the power of peer pressure. It's an experience that I don't care to repeat! At the end of the day, I asked myself the following questions:

- How would it be to have to wear this brand of pants all the time?
- How can the brand of pants change the public's opinion of your personality or character?
- Do the looks I give people have the same effect on them that everyone's did today?
- I am a high school senior, president of the Madrigal Singers, president of the debate society, member of the student council, and I just won the grand prize in our school talent show. Would I have received these honors had I worn these blue jeans every day?

I learned again that peer pressure is real and it is very powerful. Dan went into the experience very reluctantly and afraid of how he would be perceived. He let the crowd intimidate him and had a negative experience that he never wanted to repeat. Now fast forward many years to an Especially for Youth session held at Indiana University where I was asked to teach. Since my topic was peer pressure, I shared Dan's story and I asked the large group if any of them would wear a pair of cheap, unstylish jeans to school for $100. As expected, almost every hand in the room shot up. I have learned it is easy to be brave when a theoretical situation is posed and you don't think it's real. I noticed that a boy named Elden was raising his hand, which was perfect. He was the one I wanted up front because of his confidence and good looks. He was well dressed, an athlete, a piano player, and popular with the other youth. I invited him up on stage to stand in front of hundreds of his peers. I then asked him if he would wear the cheap jeans to school on the first day of school. Reluctantly, he said yes with the help of a cheering crowd. Of course, it wasn't real so it was still relatively easy to be brave. Then with a smile I told him it was his lucky day because I had the jeans with me.

I pulled out the same ugly light blue twill fabric jeans that Dan wore many years before. He looked a little nervous as we went from pretend to reality. I asked him again if he would do it. The large and spacious crowd cheered loudly for his affirmative answer. He finally agreed to wear them on the first day of school. I then explained how I wanted him to wear a complete outfit and pulled out a shirt for him to wear. It was an old yellow Cub Scout shirt and scarf that my wife had worn in her Church calling years before. I didn't have a men's shirt, plus I wanted to make him as uncomfortable as possible to make my point. Elden looked more apprehensive, but the crowd's cheers moved him to say he would do it. I was surprised. I thanked him and told him that he could return to his seat. I then told the group that I really did not expect Elden to follow through with this experiment because it would probably be social suicide to wear that outfit to school. The crowd was disappointed that I let him off the hook.

A few weeks later, back in Texas, I got a call from Indiana. It was Elden. He told me that the first day of school was coming up soon and he really wanted to wear the jeans and Scout shirt to begin the new school year. I couldn't believe he was serious. I reminded him of the bad experience Dan had when he wore them, but Elden insisted, saying he wanted to see the reaction of his classmates. I ended up sending him the pants and shirt in the mail. A few weeks later, I got the pants and shirt back with this letter.

Hey Brother Wright,
I thought I would report on how today went. If I were to sum it up in one line, I would have to say it went surprisingly well. I was kind of worried about it the night before but then I just went to school and tried to be as confident as I could and just smile and act normal . . . and it worked. A lot of people saw me, laughed, and said, "Hey, cool shirt" or something, and a lot of my friends asked why I was wearing that or if I was an Eagle and I just replied that I was "trying to spread scout spirit," and then they laughed some more.

Most people didn't say anything to me for the most part. My bishop taught me that when you are doing what's right and you have the Spirit with you, then you can be more confident in all aspects of your life. I think going to school today with the idea that I needed to be as confident as I could really helped. Mainly it was just my attitude that made the difference. The other boy [Dan] that did this was ashamed to wear them. I just smiled at people laughing at me and tried not to care what they thought of me.

This experience actually reminds me of a scripture about being a member of the Church that I think is a good example of why my attitude made a difference. The scripture is Romans 1:16. It says: "For

I am not ashamed of the gospel of Christ: for it is the power of God unto salvation to everyone that believeth." I guess what I learned from this is if we have the right attitude and aren't ashamed, people will respect that. The other moral for everyone is to just be yourself and be grateful that you are a member of the Church of Jesus Christ. On top of that, don't care what other people think of you. It'll make life easier. Besides, it only really matters what a few people make of you—yourself and the Lord—that what matters most.

Thank you for letting me borrow the outfit. It was an interesting experience and actually really surprised me and helped me to look at things differently. Plus, I'll always remember to be more careful about judging people by the way they look.

Thanks again,

Elden

The day I received his letter was very meaningful for me. Elden taught me so many lessons from his experience. First, it's important to act confident, normal, and to just smile when going against the crowd. Second, by having the right attitude, we can show that we are not ashamed of our position and people for the most part will respect that. Finally, Elden made a great point that we should not let what others think of us matter. If we are true to ourselves and to the Lord, that is all that really matters.

Challenge:

Starting today, use two memory cues per day and concentrate deeply to recall experiences you have had or that others have had with the topics. Once something comes to mind, immediately write it down in a three-word format using a person, place, or thing to distinguish it from all other possible experiences. If you focus on two subjects per day, you can go through all of them in 300 days. If you were to average three memories for each topic, you would have 1,800 experiences recalled and recorded in the three-word format in less than a year. In time you would be able to recall just about every important lesson you have ever learned in life. I promise you that if you will accept this challenge, it will help you make each day meaningful.

Notes

1. "Concerning Hurry and Leisure," *Fraser's Magazine for Town and Country*, Vol. LX, July to Dec. 1859, 147.

2. James M. Barrie, "The Rectorial Address," Delivered at St. Andrew's University, May 3, 1922.

3. "Concerning Hurry and Leisure," 148.

CHAPTER 13
Writing Your Autobiography

Spencer W. Kimball: "Your journal is your autobiography, so it should be kept carefully. You are unique, and there may be incidents in your experience that are more noble and praiseworthy in their way than those recorded in any other life. There may be a flash of illumination here and a story of faithfulness there; you should truthfully record your real self and not what other people may see in you."[1]

The first time that I read the *Autobiography of Parley P. Pratt,* I was spellbound by his personal experiences as a participant in the Restoration. His description of Joseph Smith rebuking the foul-mouthed guards while chained in a dungeon in Missouri is a timeless example of the power of personal righteousness: "He ceased to speak. He stood erect in terrible majesty. Chained, and without a weapon; calm, unruffled and dignified as an angel, he looked upon the quailing guards, whose weapons were lowered or dropped to the ground; whose knees smote together, and who, shrinking into a corner, or crouching at his feet, begged his pardon, and remained quiet till a change of guards."[2]

Since reading Pratt's story, I have gravitated toward books and talks where the authors and speakers emphasize their messages by sharing personal experiences and lessons learned. Another book that sparked my imagination was *Wilford Woodruff: History of His Life and Labors* by Matthias F. Cowley. It contains excerpts from the detailed journals President Woodruff kept. Church historians have relied heavily on those journals. The following is his account of a few days during his mission to the South in 1834:

In the southern part of Missouri and the northern part of Arkansas, in 1834, there were very few inhabitants. We visited a place called Harmony Mission, on the Osage River, one of the most crooked rivers in the West. This mission was kept by a Presbyterian minister and his family. We arrived there on Sunday night at sunset. We had walked all day without anything to eat, and were very hungry and tired. Neither the minister nor his wife would give us anything to eat, or let us stay over night, because we were Mormons, and the only chance we had was to go twelve miles farther down the river, to an Osage Indian trading post kept by a Frenchman named Jereu; and the wicked priest who would not give us a piece of bread lied to us about the road, and sent us across the swamp, where we wallowed knee-deep in mud and water till ten o'clock at night, in trying to follow the crooked river. We then left the swamp and put out into the prairie, to lie in the grass for the night.

When we got out of the swamp, we heard an Indian drumming on a tin pail and singing. It was very dark, but we traveled toward the noise, and when we drew near the Indian camp quite a number of large Indian dogs came out to meet us. They smelled us, but did not bark or bite. Soon we were surrounded by Osage Indians, and were kindly received by Mr. Jereu and his wife who was an Indian. She gave us an excellent supper and a good bed, which we were thankful for after the fatigue of the day.

As I laid my head upon my pillow, I felt to thank God from the bottom of my heart for the exchange from the barbarous treatment of a civilized Presbyterian priest to the humane, kind, and generous treatment of the savage Osage Indians. May God reward them both according to their desserts!

We arose in the morning, after a good night's rest. I was somewhat lame, from wading in the swamp the night before. We had a good breakfast. Mr. Jereu sent an Indian to see us across the river, and informed us that it was sixty miles to the nearest settlement of either white or red men.

We were too bashful to ask for anything to take with us to eat; so we crossed the river and started on our day's journey of sixty miles without a morsel of food of any kind. We started about sunrise and crossed a thirty-mile prairie, apparently as level as a house floor, without shrub or water. We arrived at timber about two o'clock in the afternoon.

As we approached the timber, a large black bear came out towards us. We were not afraid of him, for we were on the Lord's business, and had not mocked God's prophets as did the forty-two wicked children who said to Elisha, "Go up thou bald head," for which they were torn by bears. When the bear got within eight rods of us he sat on his haunches, looked at us a moment, and ran away; and we went on our way rejoicing.

We had to travel in the night, which was cloudy and very dark, so we had great difficulty to keep the road. Soon a large drove of wolves gathered around, and followed us. They came very close, and at times it seemed as though they would eat us up. We had materials for striking a light, and at ten o'clock, not knowing where we were, and the wolves becoming so bold, we thought it wisdom to make a fire; so we stopped and gathered a lot of oak limbs that lay on the ground, and lit them, and as our fire began to burn the wolves left us.

As we were about to lay down on the ground—for we had no blankets—we heard a dog bark. My companion said it was a wolf; I said it was a dog; but soon we heard a cowbell. Then we each took a firebrand, went about a quarter of a mile, and found the house, which was sixty miles from where we started that morning. It was an old log cabin, about twelve feet square, with no door, but an old blanket was hung up in the door-way. There was no furniture except one bedstead, upon which lay a woman, several children, and several small dogs.

A man lay on the bare floor with his feet to the fireplace, and all were asleep. I went in and spoke to the man, but did not wake him. I stepped up to him, and laid my hand on his shoulder. The moment he felt the weight of my hand he jumped to his feet and ran around the room as though he were frightened; but he was quieted when we informed him we were friends. The cause of his fright was that he had shot a panther a few nights before, and he thought its mate had jumped upon him. He asked us what we wanted; we told him we wished to stop with him all night, and would like something to eat. He informed us we might lie on the floor as he did, but that he had not a mouthful for us to eat, as he had to depend on his gun to get breakfast for his family in the morning. So we lay on the bare floor, and slept through a long, rainy night, which was pretty hard after walking sixty miles without anything to eat. That was the hardest day's work of my life. The man's name was Williams. He was in the mob in Jackson County; and after the Saints were driven out, he, with many others, went south.

We got up in the morning and walked in the rain twelve miles to the house of a man named Bemon, who was also one of the mob from Jackson County. The family were about to sit down to breakfast as we came in. In those days it was the custom of the Missourians to ask you to eat even though they were hostile to you; so he asked us to take breakfast, and we were very glad of the invitation. He knew we were Mormons; and as soon as we began to eat, he began to swear about the Mormons. He had a large platter of bacon and eggs, and plenty of bread on the table, and his swearing did not hinder our eating, for the harder he swore the harder we ate, until we got our stomachs full; then we arose from the table, took our hats, and thanked him for our breakfast. The last we heard of him he was still swearing. I trust the Lord will reward him for our breakfast.[3]

What a moving personal account of one early missionary's efforts to spread the gospel. His first-person narrative is far more effective and meaningful than reading a biography in which a third party tells his or her version of the story. Perhaps to Wilford Woodruff, his entries were just normal everyday life. For me, his writings have the same impact as reading about the four sons of Mosiah on their mission to the Lamanites.

Over the years, I have encountered several people who have expressed an interest in writing books. Some of them are drawn to the subject matter of an admired historical figure. Few of them realize that their own life story might be as admirable and interesting. President Ezra Taft Benson said, "You have been born at this time for a sacred and glorious purpose. It is not by chance that you have been reserved to come to earth in this last dispensation of the fullness of times. Your birth at this particular time was foreordained in the eternities."[4] This statement from a prophet of the Lord says that *you* are an important historical figure. So why not write a book about your life and experiences. The odds are that no one else will do it. Even if someone else did write your story, it wouldn't be nearly as interesting or accurate as your version. Your book may not be picked up by a national publisher and may not become a bestseller, but it may be priceless to yourself and your posterity at the very least.

I had occasion to ask a large group if they kept a record of their life experiences. Here is one of the responses: "I am the type that starts my journal with 'this is the first day of the rest of my life.' I do well for a few days, then zippo! It is kind of like going to Church where you miss one Sunday and then two and it is easy not to go back. I think often about things that I should be writing down but too often when I do think of them I am at work or in bed. *I found a journal book that my mom had written and it is priceless.* Sorry I don't have good reasons and more sorry that I couldn't say yes."

All is not lost if you have not kept a record of past experiences. In this book, I have suggested a list of approximately six hundred memory cues to spur your memory of past events. Some of those cues refer to family members, friends, or close associates. I will use my own life and my stories to show you how easy it is to begin yours. Below is an example of an outline that I would use to write such a book about myself based on my memory cues and three-word memory prompts. In italics is a three-word summary of the experience that includes the name of an individual. Since I likely know only a few people with that name, it will help me recall only that specific experience. Following the three-word summary, I include a short description of the lesson I learned from the experience.

- *Dean Rigby English*: Teachers who build instead of criticize can inspire students to change.
- *Isaac Primary Program*: Everyone needs someone who will listen to him or her with love and respect.
- *Brad Texas A&M*: Youth who are starved for physical affection will often go seeking after it.
- *Shawn Movie Theater*: People are watching you and notice if you live what you profess to believe.
- *Nathan Birth Night*: Turning to God in prayer can bring peace and comfort in trying times.
- *Allison Israel Song*: Visiting other countries usually increases the love you have for your own.
- *Jerry Dale Carnegie*: When you stand up for what you believe in, someone will often follow.
- *Ida Dies Childbirth*: You never know when it will be the last time you have to say, "I love you."
- *Carter Tractor Stuck*: Outburst of anger can damage relationships forever and lead to a loss of respect.
- *Chesser Chicken U-Joint*: Split-second decisions can lead to a lifetime of regret, so better to think first.
- *Kevin Grandma Weeks*: Do not always assume that things are really as they appear to be.
- *Mattie Shut Out*: Getting down on yourself can make things worse than they really are.
- *Ed Basketball Coach*: One person's bad attitude can affect everyone around them.
- *Ichou PhD Student*: The Book of Mormon has the ability to change people's lives for the better.
- *Cooper Sixth Grade*: Little formal education need not doom a hard worker with ambition.
- *Naomi Almost TD*: There is always a positive side of life for those willing to look closely.
- *Shay Go Cart*: Many parents fail to teach their children but then expect good decisions.

- *Edward Two Weeks*: If you quit, chances of ever finishing what you started decrease dramatically.
- *Beulah Old People*: Those who are compassionate in life have many friends at death.
- *Elaine Father Mother*: Marry someone who will be supportive of what you believe strongly in.
- *Cooper Death Day*: Death can be a celebration when a person has lived a good, long life.
- *Reynard Minnesota Fair*: We should be aware that there are people in life who will try to deceive us.
- *Reed Bradford Harvard*: Many pass on the same mistakes that their own parents make.

With a three-word prompt and a short summary, I can then devote time to recording that lesson in detail. Here is one of the experiences expanded upon and the grand lesson I learned from it.

Dean Rigby English

My first year in college was not good for my self-esteem. English was an especially painful experience for me. My professor was merciless with his red pen on everything I turned in. It was as if he needed to show us how smart he really was. Looking back on this experience, I admit that my writing was probably not the best. But I took his class to learn how to be a better writer, not to be ripped to shreds on every paper I turned in. This teacher did far more to hurt my writing skills than he ever did to help improve them.

In 1968, I was drafted into the army and had to put college on hold. Obviously, I did nothing to improve my English skills during those two years. When I came back home, I attended Brigham Young University. Though dreading the thought, I had no choice but to take an English class. This time I had a teacher named Dean Rigby. I will never forget what he did for me. He talked to us from the first night as if we were budding writers that he was privileged to teach. He had us write a paper every week during the semester. Even though he was a very kind man, I was still terrified until I got my first paper back. I was shocked to see that it did not have one negative comment on it. Had I really gotten that much better? The next week it was the same thing. I couldn't believe how good this instructor could make you feel with his encouraging comments in the columns.

I found myself actually enjoying the experience of writing the third paper. The results were the same: nothing but positive comments. The fourth week was the same. The fifth week was just a little different. He still pointed out all of the things he liked about the paper, but then he added a couple of constructive comments like, "You may want to check your use of . . . in this sentence." He never said I was doing it wrong; he just gave me a few things to think about, which I greatly appreciated. For the next three weeks, he continued to point out the positive along with a few suggestions on how I could improve my paper. During the third month and for the rest of the semester, he continued to build me up while getting more direct and specific on how I could improve my writing. His method of teaching totally changed my attitude toward writing.

The English professor I had as a freshman was not a teacher at all. He was a writing critic. He expected me to know how to write perfectly before I came to his class and he ripped me apart because I was not at that stage. Dean Rigby was an English teacher in every sense of the word. He had obviously learned that criticism kills motivation and desire in students. A teacher's job by definition should be to teach, which means to impart knowledge and to help someone understand. "Wherefore, be faithful; stand in the office which I have appointed unto you; succor the weak, lift up the hands which hang down, and strengthen the feeble knees" (D&C 81:5). I have learned that teachers who build instead of criticize can inspire students to change.

Many of the life histories we find in the records of our recent ancestors were written from memory in the advanced years of the person's life. This scenario is typical: "I'm eighty-five years old now and my family has been begging me to write my life history, so I guess I'll do it. I was born on July 24, 1929 in Salt Lake City, Utah, the daughter of John and Mary Smith. My parents were good people and taught me well . . ." I have read several of these brief and dry life histories over the years, including a few from my own ancestors. Their theme comes straight from the creed of Sergeant Joe Friday of the old TV show *Dragnet* who always said, "All we want are the facts." While any written record is better than nothing, it doesn't have to be that way. Remembering the days of your youth from the vantage point of old age can reduce your life story to "just the facts" of a timeline. It is usually much more rewarding and productive to recall experiences and events using memory cues rather than timelines. Once a life lesson is recalled, you can narrow in on the year that it occurred based on other memory cues and then arrange your memories in sequential order. Instead of just sharing facts, we can write experiences that show how each day was meaningful.

There may be times when you do want to center your memory recall on a certain period in your timeline. For example, if you served a mission, focusing on familiar mission-era memories will bring to mind others that may have been lost temporarily. At nineteen, I was drafted into the US military and was on active duty from May of 1968 until May of 1970. When I spent time thinking about my "army years," I was able to recall fifty-six experiences that occurred in just the first six months of my two-year service. That covered the time period of my basic and advanced training and first permanent assignment. Below are the three-word summaries of these experiences.

Year: 1968

Fear Draft Letter
Fort Bliss Music
Day Draft Notice
Induction Day Houston
Officer Polk Bliss
Boy Glue Induction
Gary Friend Snub
Farrow Bed Off
Private Yelling Stupid
Airport People Mocked
Battalion Mess Hall
Sgt. Bye Wilson
Physical Kristi Birthday
Letter Sick Feeling
Request Cook MOS
Wilson Lost General
Toot Toot Punishment
Make Platoon Leader
Off-Plane Bliss
Home For Christmas
Guy Funny Hat
Forget Hat Everywhere
Parents Visit Bliss
Sam Dave Concert

Guy Cheated 500
Second Fitness 470
Green Blown Up
Cattle Trucks Sands
Mile Run Heat
Dyer First Place
Miss Meal Crawl
Lost Privileges Basic
Some Will Die
Bye Smoked Ran
Watson Rifle Over
Watson Get Up
Gas Chamber Last
Chow Mess Bivouac
KP Duty Basic
Company Clerk
Temperature Ft. Bliss
Company C Trainees
Harold Harry Davis
Seven from Vidor
Fort Ord Location
Lt. Egg Sandwich
Monterey Pop Festival
Go Home Christmas

Fort Ord Friends	By Self Dance
Jimmy Hendricks Music	Tell Everyone Hood
Don't Talk Trainees	No Car Isolated
Glue Sniffer Ord	Dance on Base
Hood No Carson	Letter from Home
Private Room Ord	

Once these summaries were put in writing, I could think of the grand lessons learned from each experience and then flesh out the details in story. I could then put them in sequential order in my autobiography. The following are two examples of how using the memory cue of my "army years" resulted in full-fledged accounts.

Fort Bliss Music: May 1968

It was a year of turmoil in the United States and in my own life. Our country was involved in a cruel conflict in Vietnam and many of our young men were being killed on the battlefield. I happened to turn nineteen that year and received the letter that I had been dreading, informing me that I was now drafted into the United States Army. My first cousin Chris, one of my best friends growing up, had been killed in the war the year before. I was very nervous about serving.

I remember the sick feeling I had the day I received the letter that said, "Greetings: You are hereby ordered for induction into the Armed Forces of the United States." But I felt even sicker the night we arrived at Fort Bliss for Basic Training. We got in late and, after being yelled at for a while, we retired to our barracks. This was a large open area lined with bunk beds on two sides. I climbed onto the top bunk around 11 p.m. I found it difficult to sleep as I lay thinking of home, family, friends, and, of course, Vietnam and death. At 4:30 the next morning, the lights in the room came on and a drill sergeant began hitting the metal railings of the bunk beds with a metal rod, making a loud noise and yelling for us to get up. I have never before or since wanted so much to be home in my own bed as I did that first morning in the army.

During those first few days, we were administered shots, issued uniforms and name tags, and filled out many forms. Later, we were taken to a large auditorium for orientation. An officer made it clear how proud we should feel to be serving in the US Army. I thought to myself, *I'm not proud to be in the US Army. I just want to be home.* Next, we watched films about our military history and previous war efforts our country had been involved in. Again, military personnel talked about how proud we should be to serve our country. No matter how much they played on my emotions, I still wanted to go home. One officer solemnly reminded us of the fact that within a few months some of us would die for our country and asked if we were ready. That didn't do a lot for my morale.

Then a strange thing happened. The curtains on the stage opened to reveal a military band. After a short introduction, the band began playing patriotic songs. At first, I hung on to the very negative feelings concerning my situation. But I did say to myself, "Okay, I do like patriotic music, but I hate army life and I want to go home." However, the longer the band played, the more I felt my attitude changing. Soon I found myself thinking, *Maybe this place isn't so bad after all. Maybe I really should be here to do my part.* By the end of the concert, as the band played "The Battle Hymn of the Republic," I thought, *You know, this isn't so bad! In fact, I think I like it here.* I even began to feel that if they sent me to Vietnam, I would be okay with it. I thought, *Why not me as much as anyone else who was sent to defend our freedom?*

As the program ended that day, I was filled with patriotism and a great love for my country. I was ready to serve wherever needed. But as we walked outside into the 105-degree El Paso heat, my homesickness and fear immediately returned. Isn't it interesting that while in the auditorium listening to music I was unafraid, but when the music stopped all my fears returned? I learned for myself that day that music is powerful. It is so powerful, in fact, that it at least temporarily altered my emotions and feelings to the point that I was not afraid to go to war—at least as long as the music was playing.

Wilson Lost General: July 1968

After several weeks of training at Ft. Bliss, Texas, we were taken for a week of bivouac (camping in tents at the White Sands Missile Range in New Mexico). It was a miserable experience and I was not a happy camper. There was not a tree as far as the eye could see. The terrain was sand and sagebrush. The temperatures were hot to the extreme and we were constantly on forced marches or crawling around in the sand. The nights were no better than the days because of the winds. My tent blew down several times and the sand got in my eyes and sleeping bag. I was serving as squad leader at that time, which meant I had to be responsible for others as well. In my company was a private whose last name was Wilson. We never knew anyone's first name because only the last name was printed over the left pocket of our uniforms.

Private Wilson was as close to the character Gomer Pile in real life as anyone could get. He would drive everyone crazy saying, "Yes, drill sergeant" or "No, drill sergeant" every time he talked to someone who was not a trainee. While we were out on bivouac the first night,

Private Wilson asked someone where the latrine toilet was. The person he asked didn't know any better than he did but pointed him the way he thought it was. About 2:00 a.m., our drill sergeant came to my tent and said that everyone in our unit needed to get up and go look for Private Wilson because he never came back from the latrine. We spent most of the night searching for him without success. He seemed to have disappeared. His absence was not highly unusual, as many soldiers went absent without leave (AWOL) during the Vietnam era.

About 10:00 that morning, we all watched as an army jeep drove up. We could see from the markings on the side that it belonged to a general. We all wondered why a high-ranking officer would come to our Basic Training area. Our answer was in the back of the jeep—our fellow trainee, Private Wilson. We wondered why he was riding around with the general. Soon our company commander was standing in front of a very angry general. We couldn't hear everything being yelled at him but understood that he was accusing the captain of incompetence for not watching Private Wilson closely enough. He told him that he'd better not let the private out of his sight for the rest of Basic Training.

It seems that after Private Wilson asked the uninformed trainee where the latrine was, he started off in that direction, attempting to find his way. Without a flashlight, he had gotten lost. He continued to wander around all night and by morning had no idea where camp was. He had roamed out onto the White Sands Missile Range, where actual tests were being conducted that day. As a precaution before any testing began, helicopters flew over the area to make sure no livestock had come onto the site. One of the pilots saw Private Wilson wandering around and called the base to report it. He was soon brought back to headquarters and ended up telling his story to the officers there. The general was so angry that he personally wanted to bring the private back to his unit.

After the general left, our captain took a ten-foot rope and tied it to the back of Private Wilson's pants. During the remainder of our Basic Training, another soldier was always assigned to walk behind him (like walking a dog) to make sure he didn't get lost. I can still visualize the image of Private Wilson going to the latrine with another private outside, holding onto the rope. Without a light to find the latrine, this trainee had wandered aimlessly around until he encountered great danger. We all need a guide in our lives if we are going to reach our destination.

By starting off with a three-word title for your experiences, you can easily arrange every incident—personally experienced, observed, or learned from others—into sequential order by approximate year.

It usually takes about twenty minutes to write an experience in detail. Some may take longer and some may take less. If you could set aside an hour every Sunday, you could write an average of three of these experiences and the lessons learned, or about 156 per year. Perhaps an even better plan would be to write one a day, which would give you 365 per year. If you could just spare twenty minutes a day, you would have the content of a fascinating book in a year. In time you could have a multi-volume set of your history and leave behind for posterity much of what you have learned in life.

I have been recording experiences and observations that taught me lessons for many years. I now have approximately 5,000 recorded in what I call my three-word journal. Over time, I have written the details of those experiences and observations and what I learned from them. All of my three-word summaries are recorded on my computer and all are backed up. I also file them by topic in addition to filing them by year. The disadvantage of having experiences filed only by year is that it is difficult to retrieve something on a specific topic. When I have a class to teach or talk to give on a topic or simply a lesson I want to share with a grandchild, I want immediate access to that story. For example, if I were teaching a class on honesty, I would go directly to that subject folder on my computer and scan the forty significant experiences filed there, looking for something that would help testify of the importance of being honest. I presently have my experiences filed under more than 200 topics. This has been a tremendous help to me and has dramatically cut down on preparation time.

By filing life experiences by year, you can leave behind a compelling life history. By creating additional topic files, you have immediate access to a goldmine of material that can be used in writing blog posts, magazine articles, family newsletters, or even material to publish a book on the subject. Early pioneer Oliver Huntington left us with this thought-provoking message: "Many times have I wished that my father had kept an account of his life, that I might look over it, and see his by-gone days, deed and fortune; and never did he make the scratch of a pen towards it, until he had seen sixty cold winters; and as yet I know but very little of his life, not enough to make any record of, although I have a very short account written, but which is beyond my reach at present, if not forever. Like men in general I presume to suppose, that I shall have a posterity; and that may;

like me; wish to know of their father's life, that they might view it, and perhaps profit thereby, or at least, have the satisfaction of knowing it. This is one object that induces me to write; that my nearest kindred, might know of their kinsman. I write also for a satisfaction to myself, to look over my past life, dates and events, and to comply with a requirement, oft repeated by the Prophet Joseph Smith, 'That every man should keep a daily journal.' "[5]

Notes

1. Spencer W. Kimball, *The Teachings of Spencer W. Kimball*, ed. Edward L. Kimball (Salt Lake City: Bookcraft, 1982), 351.

2. Parley P. Pratt, *Autobiography of Parley P. Pratt* (New York: Russell Brothers, 1874), 229.

3. Matthias F. Cowley, *Wilford Woodruff: History of His Life and Labors as Recorded in His Daily Journals* (Salt Lake City: Deseret News, 1909), 48–50.

4. Ezra Taft Benson, "To the Young Women of the Church," *Ensign*, Nov. 1986, 81.

5. Oliver B. Huntington Autobiography, BYU Special Collections, 26.

CHAPTER 14
Make Every Day Meaningful

Lorenzo Snow: "Each last day or each last week should be the best that we have ever experienced, that is, we should advance ourselves a little every day, in knowledge and wisdom, and in the ability to accomplish good. As we grow older we should live nearer the Lord each following day."[1]

I believe that there is a natural, inborn tendency in human beings to want to discover something of value. Discover has three main definitions:
- Find out about something
- Be the first to find or learn something
- To find something

This predisposition to discover is manifest in various ways. Little children love to play hide-and-go-seek, search for Easter eggs, and find what the tooth fairy left under their pillow. Researchers in the medical field constantly seek to discover cures for various diseases like cancer, AIDS, asthma, diabetics, influenza, lupus, Alzheimer's, and even the common cold. Modern day treasure hunters now work underwater, where technology allows access to previously inaccessible shipwrecks in the hopes of discovering riches. Archeologists worldwide worry to find something to compare with the Rosetta stone, Dead Sea Scrolls, Pompeii, or the King Tut tomb. Inventors seek to be the next Thomas Edison, George Westinghouse, or Alexander Graham Bell. There is something rewarding about discovering something of value.

Life can be so much more rewarding if we make meaningful discoveries. Many, however, get discouraged in the quest to find something of importance. We should remember that great discoveries are few and far between. Columbus was only able to discover America one time in his life. Alexander Fleming could only discover penicillin once. In our search for ways to discover meaning in life, we should search for ways to have meaningful days and not just great discoveries. Since we are not going to discover the cure for cancer every day, perhaps we should try to discover meaningful lessons each day of our lives and record what we learn.

James Allen, the British philosophical writer, remains a perennial bestseller and source of inspiration for motivational speakers and self-help authors. He made this thought-provoking observation: "Life is a series of lessons. Some are diligent in learning them, and they become pure, wise, and altogether happy. Others are negligent, and do not apply themselves. They remain impure, foolish, and unhappy."[2]

When we look for grand lessons each day, our journey becomes exciting and meaningful. I challenge each of us to constantly ask,"What lesson can I learn from this?" When we look closely at our daily experiences, it is amazing how we are able to discover things that would have been oblivious to us without asking questions. As we discover and learn life's grand lessons, we then begin to become "pure, wise, and altogether happy." Good luck in your quest to make every day meaningful!

Notes

1. Lorenzo Snow, *Improvement Era*, July 1899, 709.

2. James Allen, *Book of Meditations for Every Day in the Year* (New Delhi: Sterling Publications, 2008), 67.

NOTES

_____

_____

_____

_____

_____

_____

_____

_____

_____

_____

_____

_____

Notes

Notes

Notes

Notes

ABOUT THE AUTHOR

Randal Wright has been fascinated by the study of families for many years. Seeking ways to raise righteous children led to his receiving a BS and MS with emphasis in the family area and then a PhD in family studies from Brigham Young University. He worked for many years as an institute director for the Church Education System and taught at BYU in the religion department. He has written several books in the past on family topics including *Families in Danger: Protecting Your Family in an X-rated World, Building Better Homes and Families,* and *The Case for Chastity: Helping Youth Stay Morally Clean.* He has spoken across the United States, Canada, and England and has been a frequent speaker at BYU Campus Education Week and the Especially for Youth program for many years. Randal and his wife, Wendy, live in Austin, Texas, and are the parents of five children and sixteen grandchildren.